300 Correction Officers Exam
Questions and Answers

Minute Help Press
www.minutehelp.com

© 2012. All Rights Reserved.

Table of Contents

ABOUT MINUTE HELP PRESS 4

USE OF FORCE AND RESTRAINTS, WEAPONS 6

SELF-DEFENSE AND PHYSICAL CONTROL OF AN INMATE. 98

OTHER FORMS OF WEAPONS 125

GENERAL FIRST AID AND CPR 149

REPORT WRITING, SPELLING AND READING COMPREHENSION. 192

MATH SKILLS 254

CHARACTERISTICS OF A CORRECTIONAL OFFICER. 272

CRIMINAL LAW AND THE CONSTITUTION AS IT PERTAINS TO CORRECTION OFFICERS.. 296

INTAKE AND SCREENING. 375

INMATE RESPECT AND DIGNITY. 384

COURT TESTIMONY 394

MEMORY AND OBSERVATIONS. 423

SITUATIONAL REASONING 467

DIFFUSION OF HOSTILITY 477

CRIMINAL ACTIVITY AND CASE WORK WITHIN PRISONS................. 526

CRITICAL INCIDENT STRESS MANAGEMENT (CISM)........................... 560

HOSTAGE SITUATIONS 574

OCCUPATIONAL SAFETY AND HEALTH 583

SUICIDE AWARENESS AND PREVENTION 596

GANGS 618

About Minute Help Press

Minute Help Press is building a library of books for people with only minutes to spare. Follow @minutehelp on Twitter to receive the latest information about free and paid publications from Minute Help Press, or visit minutehelpguides.com.

All information is based upon generalized information and does not mean that it is pertinent to any one state or facility. Know the regulations and information pertinent to your specific jurisdiction of testing.

Use of Force and Restraints, Weapons

Is the use of force in a correctional institution the same as that of a police officer on the street?

a. Yes, both require similar considerations in the level of force utilized.
b. Yes, prisoners present a high level of risk in both scenarios.
c. No, a correctional facility is established with a more controlled environment.
d. No, the level is higher in a correctional facility as the quarters are much closer.

C. is correct

Because it is a more controlled environment it is presumed that the correctional officer is working in his domain, versus the police who are in the criminal's element.

What is meant by 'reasonableness' with regard to use of force?

a. A reasonable person would not result to using any level of force.
b. A reasonable situation occurred to require that force be utilized.
c. The entire situation, inmate attitude and officer presence did not provide for a reasonable conclusion.
d. A standard that looks at all the pertinent and known circumstances and facts to make a reasonable conclusion.

D is correct.

Reasonableness asks if all the known facts and "tools" at the officer's disposal justify use of force.

Having the availability of other officers present will do what in an escalation of force scenario?

a. Additional officers present do not improve how a situation is handled.
b. The availability of additional officers pacifies the situation through intimidation.
c. A show of force can bring calmness to the situation, not requiring escalated force.
d. Added officers to the situation will normally antagonize the combatant prisoner to more violence.

C is correct.

A concerted show of force by officers is shown to cause the aggressive inmate to rethink his position.

Is the use of force in a correctional institution considered to be an everyday event?

a. No, because inmates for the most part do not want to be in situations that may affect their time served or result in disciplinary actions.
b. Yes, as it is expected that prisoners will try to combat the officer at every situation.
c. No, as it is hardly a consideration in a controlled environment.
d. Yes, prisoners know they will not face additional consequences since they are already incarcerated.

A is correct.

As most inmates have the opportunity to have time for good behavior and do not want to jeopardize that, most will not try to instigate problems.

Why is it required in most correctional facilities to file reports when the use of force is involved? Give the most correct answer.

a. The files are kept purely for administrative reasons that may affect future use of force situations.
b. The files are the record for any litigation or administrative action.
c. The reports become a means to evaluate an officer's potential for advancement.
d. The reports are used by the facility to evaluate proper techniques utilized.

A is correct.

Although other reasons do apply, use of force reports establishes factors and issues that occurred which may effect future need for use of force.

The use of force in a correctional facility falls under what Constitutional heading?

a. 14th Amendment for Due Process.
b. 4th Amendment Reasonableness standard
c. 8th Amendment Cruel and Unusual Punishment standard
d. 1st Amendment Freedom of Expression

C is correct.

Use of force issues fall under the 8th amendment as it relates to "cruel and unusual punishment." In essence no extreme or cruel use of force may occur to handle a situation, especially to the point of "deadly force."

The use of force in correctional facilities has been deemed by many courts to be allowed in which of these manners?

a. To properly control a prisoner to a point of order.
b. To properly control a prisoner to a point of submission.
c. To break up a combative situation.
d. To the extent of punishment.

A is correct.

Courts have deemed that use of force is not to be used for any type of punishment of a crime or to gain submission. They have related it to the point that order is established.

The use of justifiable force in many correctional facilities is held in oversight by whom?

a. The shift officer in charge as they have direct focus with their officers.
b. The correctional officer on scene as he or she has direct line of sight.
c. The warden as they have been established by state statutes for the administration of levels of physical force for their facility.
d. The district Attorney's office.

C is correct.

Various states have established that the warden of a prison is to establish what constitutes justifiable force and is held accountable as well.

What is the one concept in use of force that cannot be over-emphasized?

a. Personal ability
b. Training
c. Command presence
d. Respect from the inmates.

B is correct.

The use of force requires constant and continued training to keep up on current procedures and proper technique. Courts may ask the officer what their training has been in use of force situations.

Why is use of force considered a continuum?

a. Once begun use of force is hard to stop.
b. Use of force is ever changing in its practicality.
c. There is such focus.
d. Use of force has levels of handling a situation and levels of when not to be used.

D is correct.

As expressed in the answer, a continuum means that use of force has a beginning and an end with established levels of when to use and not to use it. Once begun, there has to be a defined point of ending the use of force.

How does the receiver of the use of force play into the continuum?

a. The engaged party can halt the use of force by compliance to lawful commands.
b. They have no part in the continuum.
c. The engaged party began the situation so they have to be accountable for its end.
d. The engaged party must understand that they are responsible for all actions.

A is correct.

If use of force is applied, the inmate being engaged simply has to respond properly to the command orders as the force is being used. Once they stop resisting and being combative, the officer is expected to immediately desist on the use of force.

Along with a reasonableness standard on the part of the officer, what other mindset should be at play?

a. That the use of force must never become personal revenge.
b. That use of force must always be controlled.
c. That use of force is simply to regain the inmate's respect.
d. Both A and B are correct.

D is correct.

As mentioned, use of force requires that the officer be in complete self-control and is not doing a use of force procedure to inflict punishment or performing the use of force as a revenge for the situation. They must remain professional.

Corrections officers must use levels of force escalation based on what criteria? Give the best answer.

    a. The situation where staff and other prisoners are in imminent threat of bodily injury or even death.
    b. The situation requires officers to use levels of force that are equal to the threat being posed against them.
    c. Rules and procedures that establish the appropriate level of force to be used.
    d. The situation will differ each time requiring appropriate levels of force, if needed.

C is correct

Each jurisdiction has rules and procedures in place that outline how use of force is to be utilized. Although the other answers are true, the best answer is in regards to established procedures that relate to use of force to protect the officer and the facility.

"Deadly Force" is where a substantial risk of what will occur?

a. Risk of serious bodily injury will occur, but not death.
b. Risk where serious bodily injury or death will occur.
c. Risk where only death is considered to occur.
d. Simply a phrase used in the escalation of force.

B is correct.

Deadly force is defined as force that, if used, has a high likelihood of causing serious bodily injury or even death to the party having the force applied to them.

What is considered as "acceptable levels of force"?

a. Force that falls within federal and Constitutional guidelines.
b. Force that falls within state guidelines.
c. Force that falls within departmental guidelines.
d. All of the above.

D is correct.

"Acceptable levels of force" have various rules and regulations with regard to its use. Constitutional protections, state penal codes and jurisdictional authorities have guidelines in place for what are considered to be these levels.

The Fourth Amendment standard with regard to use of force is what when a person is in custody rather then being free?

a. A subjective reasonableness standard
b. The Eighth amendment applies.
c. This amendment does not apply to use of force.
d. It becomes both subjective and objective.

B is correct.

The Eighth Amendment is what relates to the use of force. As mentioned the "cruel and unusual" punishment aspect relates to "deadly force."

In the scenario above how does it apply to Corrections officers?

a. It does not apply as it is for a peace officer making an arrest.
b. It applies in any situation to make this level of force.
c. It applies only if the inmate is threatening to escape.
d. It does not apply as it does not fit that amendment

A is correct.

The Fourth Amendment relates to the protections with regard to "search and seizure" requirements for someone being arrested from a position of loss of freedom. In correctional facilities that standard does not apply as the person facing arrest is already in a position of lost freedom.

What is an important consideration when applying the use of force?

a. The continued use of lessened force.
b. The continued presence of verbal commands.
c. The constant presence of other officers.
d. There is no practical consideration.

B is correct.

In the application of use of force, verbal commands must be used. The Standard phrase, "stop resisting" is the verbal command used to gain the struggling inmate's submission.

In the question above, why is the correct answer necessary for consideration?

a. The use of lessened force precludes need to increase.
b. The use of verbal commands places a constant reminder on the part of the inmate to respond properly.
c. The constant presence of other officers means the application of force will not continue when its effectiveness no longer exists.
d. There is no practical consideration.

B is correct.

Verbal commands place the responsibility upon the inmate to end the use of force. If they ignore the verbal commands and continue the fight, the use of force scenario may continue.

Writing a report on the use of force involved is important. Why?

a. To have an authoritative record.
b. To have a means of estimating what could have been done differently for future situations.
c. To provide a record of the event.
d. To set forth the truth in case of court proceedings.

B is correct.

Use of force reports will relate what transpired to bring on the use of force and how it was applied. This information becomes facts and factors to consider in relation to possible future use of force scenarios.

How does the officer complete a report on the use of force?

a. Only tell the minimum amount of information to complete the report.
b. Recount the event from all officers present.
c. Simply tell the truth.
d. Be as visual and descriptive as necessary.

C is correct.

This is a report of facts. All that is needed and required is the truth of the situation.

What is important for an officer when using levels of force?

a. Having had proper training to handle the use of force scenario.
b. Having understood that his use of force may be used against him in a court proceeding.
c. Remembering to be focused on just the object of his use of force.
d. Establishing the fact that the use of force is the best deterrent to situations.

A is correct.

As with all procedures proper training is a necessity. Because of the possibility of litigation that might come from the situation, the type and consistency of use of force training is a must.

In writing the use of force report, what other factors should be acknowledged?

a. If the other inmates became involved in any way.
b. If threats or verbal intimidation was used on either part.
c. If any form of weapon became involved.
d. All of the above.

D is correct.

The report is to present pertinent information. The exactness and completeness of the report will factor into disciplinary issues on those inmates involved and any possible legal issues.

What is the first thing to consider in the use of force with a riot?

a. Establishing the communication with the rioters.
b. Setting an immediate perimeter to maintain control.
c. Presenting a show of force in numbers.
d. Calling in the National Guard.

A is correct.

The rioters need to understand their presence and position will not be ignored. Communication helps to clarify the position of the officers and that consequences will occur if the rioters do not cease and desist from their position.

What are the best verbal commands to give in a riot situation?

a. Prolonged commands.
b. Short and to the point.
c. Positive commands.
d. B and C are correct.

D is correct.

Commands need to be direct so the rioters have no confusion of where the officers stand and what is expected. The commands are positive as in there will be consequences for actions committed and commands not adhered to.

What does it mean to remain disciplined for officers in a riot situation?

a. Means to establish the fact that inmates will be disciplined when the riot is over.
b. Means to discipline fellow officers that break ranks.
c. Means to remain focused in the assigned responsibility and not waver.
d. Means to set a disciplined tone with the riot group.

C is correct.

Each officer has a placement for the riot situation. By staying tuned to their primary task and not trying to do other things, the officers present a united front to the situation.

Sometimes if force is needed with a riot situation, the use will be different than with a single party. Why?

a. Harder to use force on a rioting group.
b. The way you apply the force will be watched by the non-participants.
c. Use of force requires a more lethal approach.
d. A rioting crowd makes it hard to use force to calm them down.

B is correct.

Other inmates watch how their fellow inmates are being handled in riot situations. They may try to become part of the problem if they feel their peers are being treated cruelly or unfairly. They may begin to lose respect for particular officers that resort extreme measures when dealing with rioters.

When does the use of force cease with a rioting group?

a. The moment compliance and order is restored.
b. The moment the inmate stops verbally abusing all involved.
c. After 15 minutes of use.
d. The moment the officer feels it is best to cease.

A is correct.

The same as with a single party use of force scenario. When the rioters comply with the commands to stop resisting or to break up their group.

This is the point order becomes restored.

The use of any restraint, including handcuffs, is not to be used for what scenario? Give the best answer.

a. Not to be used for purposes of safety for others around the prisoner.
b. Not to be used for purposes of punishment.
c. Not to be used for purposes of retaliation.
d. B and C are correct.

D is correct.

Restraints have specific uses and they do not include punishment or retaliation. No response to an unruly or problem inmate is to include punishment or retribution.

How long a period of time should restraints be used when they are of necessity?

a. Up to 15 minutes to control the situation.
b. No more than an hour, as that is the length of time most situations will be diffused.
c. Up to the determination of the convening authority on their discretion.
d. Only for as long as the situation requires their use.

D is correct.

Once the situation no longer requires use of a restraint, the legal qualifier is that it must be removed.

The use of leg restraints and belly chains are used in what type of situation? Give the best answer.

a. Can be used for women prisoners that are pregnant.
b. Are used appropriately and in the least restrictive manner.
c. Are to be used for all medical considerations.
d. May be used to punish a prisoner following any prescribed incident.

B is correct.

Each restraint has a proper way of being applied to the inmate and must not restrict that movement to anything unsafe or harmful.

When transporting a prisoner, most states have determined what about the use of restraints? Give the best answer.

a. One officer is plenty to properly restrain the prisoner being transported.
b. Always apply the restraints from the front so as to see the prisoner's movements.
c. Restraints need to be as reasonably tight as possible to maintain a submissive posture from the prisoner.
d. Belly chains are to be used all the time when transporting a prisoner.

D is correct.

Belly, or waist, chains are used by having the prisoners handcuffed to the waist chain. It is used during transport of the inmate to keep inmate and officer protected.

The US Supreme Court found in Hope v Pelzer that the use of restraints had to fall into which of these reasons?

a. Does the restraint solve the problem?
b. Does using the restraint answer a reasonable justification?
c. Does the restraint fulfill a current need?
d. Both b and c are correct.

D is correct.

As mentioned before about reasonable justification, the finding of the court was that using restraints must have reasonable factors and circumstances that justify their use, and that a current need was being fulfilled with the restraint use.

What constitutes reasonable justification?

a. When all other methods fail.
b. The inmate's attitude and situation establishes the need.
c. The officer's awareness to the mood present.
d. None of the above.

B is correct.

The inmate's attitude and mood, along with factors within the situation would establish the reasonable justification part of a restraint being utilized.

When is it acceptable for corrections officers to apply the use of 4-point and 5-point restraints?

a. Only after the use of lesser restraints has been proven ineffective for maintaining safety of all present and only as a last resort.
b. It is acceptable at any time.
c. It is used in unison with other restraints, such as leg irons.
d. These forms of restraints are never used in correctional facilities.

A is correct.

Because of the nature of these types of restraints and how confining the restraints are; their use becomes a last resort use if all other methods fail.

Which of these is true regarding the use of belly, or waist chains?

a. They are to be worn under the prisoner's garments so as not to be seen by the general public.
b. They are to be locked in the front so as to have ease of access in case of extreme situations.
c. The lock is to be in the rear so as not to impede their removal.
d. The chain is to sit above the navel.

C is correct.

Besides the back being the least impeded point of accessing the belly chain lock, it also prevents the inmate from directly attacking the officer, as he cannot see the officer.

Which group(s) falls under the classification of special needs group in relation to not using restraints in prisons?

a. Female prisoners that are pregnant.
b. Prisoners under the age of 18 or senior citizens.
c. Prisoners with special health considerations.
d. All of the above.

D is correct.

Because of the nature of restraints and their use, courts have found that pregnant inmates can be physically harmed, as well as their unborn child, by using restraints. Special health factors, juveniles and the elderly also have fallen into court decisions about the use of restraints.

Double-locking a set of handcuffs means what?

a. Means that two sets of handcuffs are used for double securement.
b. Means that the handcuffs have 2 points of locking mechanism.
c. There is no such practice.
d. Means that the officer double locks the handcuffs so that the ratchet does not slide on the cuffs.

D is correct.

By turning the lock both ways in handcuffs, the ratcheting mechanism will not slide.

When should the use of restraints be used on a pregnant woman?

a. Never
b. Only when officer safety is an issue.
c. Depends on the trimester the woman is in.
d. Used only as a means to aid in the inmate's welfare.

A is correct.

As mentioned before, courts have found pregnant women to be exempt from the use of restraints.

Another restraint found with many correctional facilities is a shock belt. What is important about it?

a. It is used by many facilities when transporting maximum security prisoners to court.
b. It is not a recommended form of restraint.
c. It is used to control resistant inmates.
d. None of the above.

A is correct.

Shock, or stun, belt gives an electrical shock to inmates that might become a danger to others in court rooms. The shock occurs when a correctional officer pushes a button on a remote that delivers the shock. This allows for maximum security level inmates to be held in control while in the courtroom.

Correctional officers have certain policies with regard to firearms, differing from police. Why?

a. Being in close quarters to the prisoners, the storing and carrying of firearms is different.
b. Firearms are not used in prison facilities.
c. Firearms in correctional facilities are present to offer a form of deterrent.
d. None of the above.

A is correct.

Police officers are in free space and making arrests. Correctional officers are dealing with people already without freedom and in close confines with inmates. Wearing firearms around inmates increases risks of an inmate getting hold of a firearm.

Correctional officers may carry firearms in which of these circumstances?

a. When transporting a prisoner outside of the facility or watching inmates working outside of the facility.
b. When conducting head counts in the lockdown environment.
c. When breaking up an altercation.
d. When serving meals, as this puts the officer in close proximity to the prisoner.

A is correct.

Since the correctional officer is not inside the facility and the distance between them and inmates has increased, the validity for carrying a firearm is present.

Why are county corrections officers allowed to have firearms and not state?

a. It is not a true statement.
b. Only some county officers can, as they are also deputized and have police powers.
c. Neither can have firearms.
d. It depends on each jurisdiction.

D is correct.

Each state and jurisdiction has their own regulations. Some county correctional facilities are manned by sworn peace officers and some jurisdictions are privatized.

Are correctional officers that have access to or use of firearms required to pass qualifying for marksmanship?

a. It is not deemed necessary as the officer rarely will use a firearm.
b. Just as with police, qualifying is still considered a requirement.
c. Only for the sake of record keeping.
d. None of the above.

B is correct.

Officers that are allowed to carry firearms need to show they have the skill and marksmanship to handle a firearm, similar to sworn peace officers.

The use of chemical agents is appropriate in what circumstance?

a. As a part of the escalation of restraint use.
b. When all other parts of the conflict resolution have been exhausted.
c. In tandem with other conflict resolution techniques.
d. There is no such form of conflict resolution.

B is correct.

These agents fall under the use of force continuum and have their respective level of authorized usage.

Is tear gas still used with regard to handling correctional facility riots?

a. No
b. In limited use.
c. It is an authorized means of dismantling a riot.
d. It is the first action taken.

C is correct.

Tear gas is still in use and allowed in handling riots when deemed appropriate.

Self-Defense and Physical Control of an Inmate.

Different states have accepted self-defense techniques that they are authorized to teach their corrections officers. It is incumbent upon the student to become familiar with accepted practices and training appropriate to the techniques.

Why is the open-hand method the most common form of self-defense?

a. It is considered to be the least lethal to an inmate.
b. It is least recognized by inmates.
c. It allows for personal protection to the officer, while making necessary strikes on the inmate.
d. It is the easiest to learn.

A is correct.

Open hand method establishes least possibility of serious injury or lethal result if applied correctly from training. If it is not accomplishing its intended result, the next step in the continuum would be utilized.

Some agencies use PPCT. What is it?

a. PPCT is an outdated form of self defense.
b. PPCT is Pressure Point Control Technique, which focuses on particular muscle pressure points.
c. PPCT is Passive Placed Control Technique that allows for unconscious producing holds.
d. PPCT is Post Partum Control Technique.

B is correct.

PPCT is an authorized form of arrest control by many departments. It focuses on 13 known pressure points on the human body to gain submission from the intended target.

How does PPCT work when a prisoner is resisting handcuffing?

a. It is a maneuver of a pressure point behind the neck.
b. It is used as an inward curl of the arm to apply pressure.
c. It is used as a brachial stun.
d. It is used as a jaw line pressure point.

B is correct.

One aspect of PPCT is to use leverage and proper manipulation of bending an arm to apply pressure. This pressure causes certain motor functions in the person to be affected and resistance to handcuffing is taken away.

Another form of self-defense training used by certain correctional facilities in the U.S. is called Krav Maga. How does it work?

a. It responds to opponent's combative motions.
b. It is just another martial art.
c. It uses body instincts and motion.
d. It is a matter of mind over matter.

C is correct.

Krav Maga uses the initiator's body movements and instincts to come into play. The one using the Krav technique responds with motions and grabs according to the attacks being made against him or her. They become instinctive with proper training.

Where does Krav Maga originate?

a. It came from Israel.
b. It came from South Africa.
c. It came from Russia.
d. It came from China.

A is correct.

It is an Israeli originated form of self-defense.

The art of Koga training introduced what important facet into law enforcement and corrections?

a. A way of applying baton strikes.
b. A way of using hand to hand combat.
c. A way of consistent pressure on an opponent.
d. A way to handle verbal situations.

A is correct.

The creator of Koga training of self-defense established a means of using baton strikes to combat resistance of the aggressor.

What constitutes a situation requiring self defense?

a. Self –defense is used when an inmate is disregarding proper commands.
b. Self-defense is used when a prisoner has become combative.
c. Self-defense is not a recognized corrections procedure.
d. Each situation is different and the necessity for self-defense is reflective of each situation.

B is correct

Self-defense is used to prevent injury to the officer when an inmate becomes physically combative. When verbal commands have become ineffective and the aggressor initiates physical attacks, then self-defense methods become permissible.

What is a general definition of self-defense?

a. The ability to resist an attack.
b. The ability to protect against and resist a combative enemy.
c. The ability to proactively subdue the combatant.
d. The ability to resist and subdue the combatant.

B is correct.

Self-defense is as it sounds. To protect oneself from the attacks of an aggressor and resist his attacks to avoid receiving personal injury or death.

To use self-defense is to have self-control of situations. What does this mean?

a. The control necessary to prevent the situation from escalating.
b. The control one exhibits to regulate movement of all participants.
c. The ability to properly exert enough influence over an inmate to keep the situation safe.
d. The control one has by using manual implements to maintain the situation.

C is correct.

Self-control in self-defense means the officer instinctively responds with controlled movements and motions to protect himself and to keep from injuring the aggressor beyond what would be reasonable.

What is the most important way to use self-defense properly?

a. Alertness and control.
b. Stand with obvious pride.
c. Maintain an intimidating presence.
d. Establish the rules and regulations from the beginning.

A is correct.

To use self-defense properly, the officer must have control of the situation at all times. By being alert, the officer can respond appropriately to what attacks are happening and how the aggressor is responding to the level of defensive maneuvers.

How do personal prejudices affect a situation?

a. They can alienate the inmate with a feeling of being made inferior.
b. They can establish a mindset where there is no room for the inmate to maneuver in situations.
c. They can set in motion situations of conflict.
d. They are necessary in correctional facilities.

C is correct.

How an officer views the inmates and how he or she treats them will have a great influence. If the officer has established prejudices, such as race, sexual orientation or others, and makes them apparent to inmates, the inmates are likely to grow uneasy and possibly feel threatened at some point.

Why does an officer need to know self-defense?

a. It is an officer's duty to show the inmates he has the ability to win in a combatant situation.
b. The officer will never be in a situation requiring self-defense if he follows the rules.
c. Self-defense gives the officer a feeling of security that he can handle any situation.
d. Self-defense is exactly as it says, to defend oneself and to come out of a situation with no serious wounds or life threatened.

D is correct.

If the officer does not know how to defend him or herself they become easy targets for aggression and intimidation. By knowing sound self-defense practices, the officer increases his or her likelihood of walking away from an attack with little to no injury.

The proper way to approach an inmate when placing on handcuffs is to what?

a. Come directly from their front so they can see your intent.
b. Come directly from the back.
c. Come from their back and slightly from the side, and told to have eyes face front, to prevent their knowing where you are exactly.
d. None of the above.

C is correct.

By applying handcuffs from the rear and off-set to the side, the inmate has lost the advantage of becoming resistant or aggressive. This happens because the inmate does not see the position of the officer applying the handcuffs.

Other Forms of Weapons

This is another situation where each state has its own guidelines on whether a corrections officer is allowed to carry weapons, such as pepper spray and batons. Become familiar with your particular jurisdiction.

To use pepper spray, one must be aware of its ingredients. What is it?

a. Resin from finely ground chili peppers.
b. Resin from finely ground onions.
c. It is a synthetic chemical.
d. It is a combination of finely ground varieties of peppers.

A is correct.

Pepper spray ingredients are resins from ground chili peppers.

Pepper spray, or OC spray, is measured in Scoville Units. What does this mean?

a. It is a unit to measure the size of the pepper grounds.
b. It measures the "hotness" of the ingredient.
c. It is another word for volume.
d. It measures the length of exposure to the ingredient.

B is correct.

Scoville measurements are used to measure the "hotness" of peppers. It is why OC, or pepper spray, is measured by means of Scoville Units.

Which is the most common form of propellant for dispersing the OC?

a. Nitrogen
b. Various gases
c. Hydrocarbon formula
d. Carbon Dioxide

C is correct.

Although the others listed are proper ways of dispersing, Hydrocarbon formula is the most commonly used form of propellant.

When pepper spray is applied what is the most distinctive reaction?

a. Eyes begin to water and dilate.
b. Mouth starts to dry up.
c. The skin color will change to a light blue.
d. The nose will begin to infuse.

A is correct.

The effects of pepper spray, the ground chili pepper resin, are to cause the eyes to tear and dilate.

To administer Pepper Spray properly, what should a corrections officer be aware of?

a. That the inmate may become combative further if not enough OC was applied.
b. The officer should undergo a test of Pepper spray application personally to understand its effects.
c. There are no special considerations for the use of Pepper Spray.
d. The effects will be the same for all inmates that have been sprayed.

B is correct.

Many correctional facilities require their officers to undergo pepper spray applications so as to have a better understanding of its effects. In courtrooms, lawyers have asked officers that applied pepper spray if they have personal experience and training in its use.

Why must there be records maintained of all OC uses?

a. To protect the officer and facility in case of litigation.
b. Required by law.
c. Must have a use to properly handle inventory.
d. To keep a medical account so as not to administer the OC too often on any one inmate.

A is correct.

Just as with use of force, pepper spray use can bring on litigation. By having a properly filled out record of its use, it can be used as evidence on behalf of the correctional facility and its officers.

If applying Pepper spray, what should the officer be doing?

a. Make sure to make audible and loud commands for the inmate to submit to the command.
b. Be in as close as possible to properly administer.
c. Keep your own eyes closed so as not to get overspray.
d. Always administer alone so as not to affect other officers.

A is correct.

As with other use of force scenarios, pepper spray must be ceased when the target becomes compliant. This is done by verbally commanding the inmate to stop resisting.

When using a baton which of these is the most serious consideration?

a. The length of the baton as it will create or lesson distance between officer and the inmate.
b. The composition of the baton so as to prevent it from becoming broken.
c. The proper use from having had prescribed training.
d. Knowing where to make the most effective strikes on the inmate.

C is correct.

Baton use requires that the officer receive proper training. When properly trained, the officer should use the baton appropriately and when necessary.

In the above question, which becomes a secondary consideration?

a. The length of the baton as it will create or lesson distance between officer and the inmate.
b. The composition of the baton so as to prevent it from becoming broken.
c. The proper use from having had prescribed training.
d. Knowing where to make the most effective strikes on the inmate.

D is the correct answer.

Baton strikes can only be made at certain points of the inmate. Knowing these points maintains the proper use and will not inflict unnecessary injury to the inmate.

The length of the baton is important for what reason?

a. The length should match the size of the officer using the baton.
b. The length allows for proper distance between the officer and the inmate.
c. The length is of no consideration.
d. The length becomes the preference of the officer using the instrument.

B is correct.

Proper baton length will keep the officer safely away from the inmate if he or she should become more aggressive. The distance allows for the proper strike to be made and to protect the officer from becoming the victim.

Where in the escalation of force continuum do impact weapons such as batons fall in regards to their place of use?

a. During the hand-applied force.
b. Just after the hand-applied force is not bringing results.
c. Used in place of hand-applied force.
d. It is not used; it simply goes directly to deadly force if hand-applied fails.

B is correct.

In the use of force continuum, most correctional facilities place baton strikes as the next step if hand-applied force is not working.

What is the most commonly used type of baton?

a. A side-handle baton.
b. A telescopic baton
c. A flashlight
d. A straight-club

B is correct.

The telescopic baton allows for an easy carrying short baton to become a long one in a single motion of the wrist. When not being used it can be retracted and placed back into its carrying holster.

General First Aid and CPR

Some questions relate to specific first-aid scenarios and other general topics.

Why is it important for corrections officers to know first-aid and CPR?

a. The officer is often the first responder.
b. The officer has the best training.
c. The officer has the capacity to perform medical services.
d. The officer has the most contact with the inmates.

A is correct.

As the first responder, the officer can begin proper first-aid or CPR. It is required that an officer be certified in these disciplines and as such will usually be the first one on the scene within correctional facilities.

Many facilities require officers to carry tactical first-aid kits. Why?

a. The kit may be the only first aid available in the prison.
b. The officer has access to immediate equipment this way.
c. The kit is not a required belt item.
d. It is better that the officer has something available, even if untrained in its use.

B is correct.

By having certain first-aid equipment immediately upon his or her person, the officer can begin to treat certain medical needs quickly and appropriately.

An inmate has suffered a burn on his arm and you have access to cool water. When do you use the water?

a. If the burn is beginning to blister.
b. If the burn is only red with no blistering.
c. For all types of burns.
d. Never use cool water to deal with burns.

C is correct.

Cool water is the prescribed first step when dealing with any form of burn that could happen in a correctional facility.

An inmate has suffered a deep gash from a fight. Why is he turning pale and breathing becomes hurried?

a. He is in shock.
b. He has lost considerable blood.
c. He is choking on something.
d. He hates the sight of blood.

A is correct.

After this type of a situation, the natural result is for a person to experience shock. Loss of blood, skin turning pale and hurried breathing are acknowledged symptoms of shock.

How do you handle a case of shock?

a. Have the inmate lie down flat on his back.
b. Have the inmate's legs elevated.
c. Loosen the clothing and keep warm.
d. All of the above.

D is correct.

The prescribed method is to lay the person on their back, elevate their feet and to keep them warm and loosen their clothing so as not to become restrictive.

A prisoner is experiencing an epileptic seizure. What should you do first?

a) Immediately check his pulse.
b) Get someone to help him remain still.
c) Try to put his head on something soft.
d) Clear room so as to prevent injury to himself.

D is correct.

When dealing with epileptic seizures, the prescribed method is to clear plenty of room so the person will not seriously injure themselves. This is because the person will have uncontrolled movement while on the ground.

If an inmate has had his face splashed with a chemical agent, what should the officer first do?

a. Take him immediately to the medical facility.
b. Try to calm the inmate down.
c. Use water to cleanse the eye area.
d. Check the chemical involved for first-aid instructions.

C is correct.

The prescribed methods are to try and rinse the eye as much as possible with water. Further treatments will follow after this measure is taken.

If an inmate suffers a burn, what is the response after a cool water bath?

a. Find burn ointment to apply.
b. Get the facility doctor or nurse to handle the situation.
c. Place dry, clean gauze on the burn area to prevent infection.
d. Do nothing to allow the burn to have air.

C is correct.

Since the burn will open the skin, placing a clean gauze on the wound will aid in preventing more dirt and particles from entering the wound.

If an officer feels an inmate has some form of internal injury, what should they do?

a. Have the victim sit up and remain calm.
b. Immediately contact emergency help.
c. Keep administering fluids to prevent dehydration.
d. Place a towel under the head while lying down.

B is correct.

The only thing the officer can do is contact immediate medical help. Internal injuries cannot be seen and must be left to medical personnel to ascertain the injury. Just keep them calm and comfortable until help arrives.

If you are checking the carotid artery for a pulse, where are you checking?

a. On the wrist.
b. On the front of the neck.
c. Behind the leg, below the knee.
d. Just up from the elbow.

B is correct.

The carotid artery is located on the front of the neck.

A fellow officer slips on the stairs and suffers a twisted ankle, what do you do?

a. Have them stand on it to see if it is injured.
b. Apply some form of cold compress.
c. Check to see if there is swelling by watching the ankle.
d. Have them sit still and stay off of the ankle.

D is correct.

Since the extent of injury cannot be seen, the officer should not be allowed to stand on the foot. Having the person sit still and not move the ankle is the first and best approach.

What are the signs of heat stroke?

a) Shallow breathing
b) Temperature does not rise.
c) Rapid pulse.
d) A and c

D is correct.

Heat stroke is known to be evidenced by a rapid pulse and hurried, shallow breathing.

An inmate has been in a knife fight and the blade is still in the arm. What do you do first?

a. Figure out the blade size to see what damage has been done.
b. Do not attempt to remove the blade, but allow medical personal to handle that procedure.
c. Slowly withdraw the blade and be ready to place on a gauze pad.
d. Apply immediate pressure to the area after removing the knife.

B is correct.

The knife damage internally cannot be seen by the officer, so removing the blade might cause further and increased damage internally. That is best left to trained medical personnel.

What is the best way to treat Dehydration?

a. Give the person immediate fluids.
b. Place a cold compress upon the person's forehead.
c. You do nothing; it is their responsibility to stay hydrated.
d. Place a warm blanket around the person.

A is correct.

Dehydration means fluids have been lost. Giving the person water will help to replenish those fluids.

CPR is what?

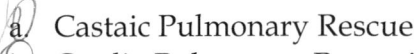

a. Castaic Pulmonary Rescue
b. Cardio Pulmonary Resuscitation
c. Contact Primary Responders
d. Means nothing, it is simply letters to represent a health practice.

B is correct.

CPR is Cardio Pulmonary Resuscitation.

In using CPR, what is the normal compressions to breath relationship?

a) 30 compressions to 1.
b) 30 compressions to 2.
c) 20 compressions to 2.
d) 20 compressions to 1.

B is correct.

The American Red Cross says that for adults 30 compressions to every 2 breaths is the prescribed way of performing proper CPR.

After making sure you have good space to work in, what is first thing to do in administering CPR?

a. Have someone contact immediate aid.
b. Check for a pulse.
c. Remove top clothing to administer CPR.
d. Check for breathing patterns.

A is correct.

It is imperative that medical personnel be contacted. Once that is accomplished by having someone do it, you can commence with CPR procedures.

What are the recommended chest compressions per minute?

a. 100
b. 80
c. 70
d. 60

A is correct.

The American Red Cross Says that 100 compressions per minute is the prescribed rate of chest compressions.

Between compressions, where should the chest position be?

a. At a full compression level.
b. At a partial chest compression level.
c. At full rest level.
d. Does not matter, just continue compressions.

C is correct.

The chest compression must begin each time at the full chest rest. That ascertains that a full compression has occurred.

Once the person is breathing on their own, what do you do?

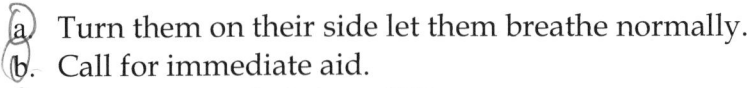

a. Turn them on their side let them breathe normally.
b. Call for immediate aid.
c. Continue to administer CPR.
d. Leave them on their back so as to maintain current breathing.

A is correct.

Turning the person onto their side is the prescribed way of allowing them to breathe on their own. CPR procedures must cease once the person is handling their own breathing.

What maneuver do you use to aid someone that is choking?

a. The Hemlock maneuver
b. The Heinrich maneuver.
c. The Heimlich maneuver.
d. The Henny maneuver.

C is correct.

The Heimlich maneuver is the proper name for aiding someone that is choking.

How does the above maneuver work?

a. Grab person around the stomach and pull in.
b. Grab the person around the stomach and thrust upwards.
c. Grab the person around the waist and thrust upwards with hands grasped.
d. Grab the person around the waist and pull inwards.

C is correct.

The prescribed way of performing the Heimlich is to grab around the waist and thrust upwards with hands grasped.

What will be the result of this maneuver?

a. The obstruction should become dislodged.
b. The obstruction will dissolve.
c. The person should vomit his or her stomach.
d. None of the above.

A is correct.

By performing this maneuver the lodged obstruction should shoot out of the throat and mouth.

Report Writing, Spelling and Reading Comprehension.

This section of questions will illustrate the need for well-written reports and for complete reports. Whether it is incident related reports or any report writing, the need for clarity and conciseness cannot be overemphasized.

What is the "who" of an incident report?

a. The officer involved.
b. The victim of an incident.
c. The party responsible for instigating the incident.
d. The witness to the incident.

C is correct.

The party that began the incident is the who of an incident report.

The incident report is a story of what?

a. The incident that occurred.
b. The findings of an incident.
c. The varying aspects of what started the incident.
d. The witness statements.

A is correct.

The incident report refers to the incident or situation that occurred justifying the writing of an incident report.

What is the importance of a good correctional incident report?

a. The report is open to review by the public.
b. The report becomes the basis for a solid or weak court case.
c. The report is merely a recall of the facts.
d. The report establishes credibility.

B is correct.

Like a police report, the incident report will be the written record of what transpired. The report being properly written can have a positive bearing on the incident review board or court case.

A good written must do what?

a. Collaborate well with any recorded versions of the incident.
b. Verify the statements of all involved.
c. Present clear facts to the incident.
d. All of the above.

D is correct.

A good report must collaborate well any recorded versions of the incident, verify all the statements made and present clear facts.

What should a report not consist of?

       a. It should not be written with clear information, only opinions.
       b. It cannot be written with officer's perspectives, only facts.
       c. It must relate witness accounts that match those of the victim.
       d. It must showcase the ability of the officer to write with sophistication.

B is correct.

The report must be written strictly with the facts, nothing else.

What can a good report do for a court case?

a. It is usually looked at as extraneous information.
b. It serves to make the DA look credible.
c. It can make or break a case.
d. It is to show the credibility of an officer.

C is correct.

A good report can bring a good or bad conclusion to a criminal proceeding.

What is one of the steps in writing a correctional institute incident report?

a. Gather all the pertinent facts ahead of time.
b. Be sure to articulate with clarity every step of the incident.
c. Witness statements are not part of the report.
d. Both a and b.

D is correct.

An incident report must include all the facts that were gathered ahead of time and have clear articulation of every step that occurred in the incident.

Why are witness statements important to the report?

a. These statements establish unbiased accounts of the incident.
b. These statements can establish a credible view of the perpetrator and the victim(s).
c. The statements allow the officer to decide who is a credible witness.
d. They have no bearing to the importance of a report.

B is correct.

Witness statements can provide a credible perspective of everyone that was involved in the incident. It may not always be the case, but if found to be false or lacking in truth the witness can face perjury charges.

Ultimately, how important is a good incident report?

a. It is important as it the only authoritative information.
b. It is somewhat important.
c. It is important only to the records department.
d. It is important as it can make or break the results.

D is correct.

Ultimately, the incident report can provide the outcome of a hearing or trial.

Answer the next few questions in relation to report writing based on the following narrative.

Two inmates were involved in a fight, brandishing knives, and they both made cuts upon each other. The prison officers were dispatched to break-up the fight and to collect evidence. The two dispatched officers placed everyone else into lockdown within their individual cells, except for the two combatants and two witnesses. With additional aid of three more officers, the fight was ended and wounds attended to. The fight occurred within the break area outside of the inmate's cell area. One witness recounted the first inmate having made a remark that insulted the other inmate, which led to the altercation. He mentioned that the knives were provided by another inmate who was in the group having been locked down. The second witness noted that the second inmate seemed to make the attack without provocation. The two combatant inmates and the knife provider were placed into solitary confinement, and the witnesses allowed to return to their cells.

Where did the incident occur?

a. It occurred in the work yard.
b. It occurred in the cell break area.
c. It occurred in the hallway outside of the cells.
d. It occurred in the cell.

B is correct.

The incident occurred in the cell break area.

How do you use and write up the witness accounts?

a.   Use only the first witness as his information was more complete.
b.   Use the second witness account only if it supports the first one.
c.   Use both and write them informally.
d.   Use neither as they are inmates and reasonably not credible.

C is correct.

Use both statements in the report as given. Do not add or subtract from what was said.

Although not mentioned in the narrative, what else should be in the report?

a. The attitude of the inmates.
b. The time of the occurrence.
c. The room description.
d. The condition of the space.

B is correct.

All incident reports must have the time the incident occurred mentioned.

How important is good English in report writing?

a. Extremely important as it establishes the credibility of the report writer.
b. Somewhat important as it relates a story.
c. Not very important as it has no bearing on the truth.
d. No importance.

A is correct.

The credibility of the report writer can be established by a solid understanding of English in reports.

In what type of handwriting are reports written?

- a. In cursive as it is a report for public use.
- b. In print as it is the easiest to read.
- c. Only done on a voice recording.
- d. It is done in short hand for others to retype.

B is correct.

Print form of hand-writing is the prescribed method for writing reports. This method is considered the most legible.

Report writing will answer what questions?

a. Who was involved?
b. Where it took place.
c. What happened?
d. All of the above.

D is correct.

The report being written must answer the questions of who was involved, where it happened and what was the incident that occurred.

11. How should a description of a person in an incident report be completed?

a. Basic facts are all that is needed.
b. As complete a description as possible so that there is no question to the correct individual being described.
c. Written with a flowery and enhanced look at the victim's description.
d. Written in academic language so as to seem professional.

B is correct.

The description that is as complete as possible will lessen the likelihood of the wrong person being described and identified.

Spelling is extremely important to report writing. The next five questions will show words that need to have the correct spelling selected.

What is the correct spelling of this word?

a. Grammer
b. Grammar
c. Gramar
d. Gramer

B is correct.

The correct spelling is Grammar.

What is the correct spelling for this word?

a. deposition
b. diposition
c. deppsettion
d. deposishion

A is correct.

The correct spelling is deposition.

What is the correct spelling for this word?

a. Incarseration
b. Incarrceration
c. Incarceration
d. Encarseration

C is correct.

The correct spelling is incarceration.

What is the correct spelling for this word?

a.   alterkation
b.   altarcashion
c.   altercashuion
d.   altercation

D is correct.

The correct spelling is altercation.

What is the correct spelling for this word?

a. delliberate
b. diliretae
c. delibearate
d. deliberate

D is correct. The correct spelling is deliberate.

Which sentence below is properly constructed grammatically?

a. The deputy and myself listened to the inmate.
b. The deputy and me listened to the inmate.
c. The deputy and I listened to the inmate.
d. The deputy and me listened to the inmate.

C is correct.

"The deputy and I listened to the inmate." is the properly constructed sentence.

Which sentence below is properly constructed grammatically?

a. The inmate's cell was searched and nothing was found.
b. The inmates cell were searched and nothing was found.
c. The inmates cells was searched and nothing was found.
d. The inmates's cell was searched and nothing was found.

A is correct.

"The inmate's cell was searched and nothing was found." is the correctly constructed sentence.

Which sentence below is properly constructed grammatically?

a. The contraband was theres and we properly handled it.
b. The contraband was theirs and we properly handled it.
c. The contraband was their's and we properly handled it.
d. The contraband was there's and we properly handled it.

B is correct.

"The contraband was theirs and we properly handled It." is the properly constructed sentence.

Answer the next set of questions based on this narrative.

When the prosecution begins their part of voir dire for selecting the jury, they will begin to ask relevant questions to the jury potentials. They may ask the individual if he or she has ever read or seen information about the case. The party may be asked their opinion of certain matters; such as belief in the death penalty, do they believe a person is influenced by their environment, if they have any knowledge of the defendant, and other pertinent information. Then the defense attorney is allowed to ask questions in relation to voir dire. For purposes of understanding, voir dire means "to find the truth" or "truth of the matter." This becomes a means by which attorneys on both sides of an argument can purge the list of nominees for the jury until they have their final selection. Anytime during the voir dire process, either attorney can ask a potential juror be excused based upon answers the party gave to questions or assessment of the person's knowledge or beliefs.

 Once the selection has been completed, then the judge will finalize the jury selection.

In the narrative, who begins the process of voir dire?

a. The defense attorney.
b. The judge
c. The prosecution.
d. The potential juror.

C is correct.

According to the narrative the prosecution begins the voir dire.

Which of these was not listed as "certain matters"?

a. Knowledge of the defendant.
b. Knowledge of criminal procedure.
c. Belief of the death penalty.
d. Are persons influenced by their environment?

B is correct.

In the narrative "knowledge of the criminal procedure" was not listed as "certain matters."

"Voir Dire" means what?

a. To tell the truth.
b. Truth exists.
c. Find the truth.
d. Nothing but the truth.

C is correct.

Voir dire means to find the truth.

In the narrative, what does the judge do?

a. Selects the jury.
b. Has no part in the process.
c. Questions all the potential jurors.
d. Finalizes the selection.

D is correct.

According to the narrative the judge finalizes the selection of jurors.

What was the first question asked of the potential juror?

a. Have you seen or read anything on the case?
b. Have you participated in the case?
c. Have you spoken with the defendant?
d. Have you any issues with the death penalty?

A is correct.

The first question asked of the potential juror was, "have you seen or heard anything on the case?"

Math Skills

Just as reading and writing is important, so are math skills within the prison system.

Following are basic math questions to help you understand the situations, such as keeping count of prisoners and other math needs.

Use the following narratives to answer the questions relating to them.

You are watching your cell block and start your day with 120 prisoners. At 9:00 a.m. 30 prisoners leave to head off to work details. Fifteen minutes later 26 come in for temporary holding as their area is being treated for bugs. At 10:30, 17 inmates leave to go to the work-out room. At Noon, 36 leave to go to the recreational area and 17 come back from work details. At 1:00 pm the 26 inmates from earlier are allowed to leave to go back to their own cells. By dinner time, 30 inmates have returned.

How many inmates are in the area by dinner time?

a. 76
b. 84
c. 82
d. 78

B is correct.

There are 84 inmates by dinner time.

How many need to return to have the original 120?

a. 36
b. 32
c. 40
d. 44

A is correct.

36 need to return to have the 120.

How many did you have at 10:30 am?

a. 95
b. 89
c. 99
d. 87

C is correct.

There were 99 by 10:30 am.

If at noon only 8 had returned, what would the count be?

a. 73
b. 67
c. 59
d. 71

D is correct.

Only 71 would be present by noon.

Each inmate is allotted one sheet, one pillow case, and one blanket. Your cell block houses 25 inmates. On day 1 each inmate turned in their used sheets, pillow cases and blankets and received new ones. On day 2, 15 inmates turned in their old ones for new ones, while the other 10 kept theirs. On day 3, all 25 turned in their old ones for new ones. On day 4, 18 turned in their old ones and received new ones, while the other seven kept theirs. On day 5, all 25 turned in old ones and received new ones.

In total by day 5, how many new sheets were distributed throughout the week?

a. 103 sheets
b. 108 sheets
c. 101 sheets
d. 107 sheets

B is correct.

108 sheets were distributed throughout the week.

From day 2 through day 4, how many pillow cases had been distributed new?

a. 58
b. 56
c. 54
d. 60

A is correct.

58 pillow cases had been distributed new.

From day 1 through day 4 how many total of everything was new?

a. 247
b. 243
c. 249
d. 241

C is correct.

There were 249 new of everything during that time.

From 4 through day 5 how many total of everything was kept?

a. 19
b. 21
c. 23
d. 25

B is correct.

21 of everything were kept total.

Characteristics of a Correctional Officer.

The next section deals with traits and characteristics of a good correctional officer. This will allow for improved relations with inmates and gaining a working trust with them.

Why is trust a good trait to have in your tactical workbox?

a. Trust establishes respect from the inmate.
b. Trust tells the inmate you have the authority.
c. Trust tells the inmate you will not be intimidated.
d. Trust is not that important in prisons.

A is correct.

Inmates respond to officers they can respect. Trust helps to establish this respect.

What trait shows the inmate that the correctional officer can be impartial?

a. Portraying an impression of preferring one over another.
b. Doing favors for those that follow the rules.
c. Not giving into special requests from any inmate.
d. By being available.

C is correct.

When inmates see that officers will not play favorites and give in to favors from certain inmates, they know the officer is an impartial person.

Clarity will perform what task in a prison environment?

a. Clarity will show that the correctional officer is focused.
b. Clarity establishes the rules that inmates must adhere to.
c. Clarity provokes others into positive action.
d. Clarity keeps everything clear and concise.

D is correct.

When things are clear and concise, then clarity has been established.

Why is personal hygiene so important for a correctional officer?

a. Cleanliness is next to godliness.
b. Personal hygiene establishes you as a professional.
c. Personal hygiene tells the inmate you are not on their level.
d. Cleanliness shows others you will not come to work filthy.

B is correct.

Inmates will respond to someone they feel is a professional in their job. Personal hygiene adds to that professionalism.

Why does a correctional officer insist on rules being followed?

a.   This tells the inmate that the guard is the ultimate authority.
b.   It establishes to the inmate that they are undeserving of fairness.
c.   It protects everyone involved.
d.   It establishes the rule of law within the facility.

C is correct.

The rules are in place to provide for safety as a primary factor. Following the rules helps maintain safety in the facility.

What is so important about the art of critical thinking?

a. It positions you as a valuable commodity to the facility.
b. It tells inmates you will not be easy mark.
c. It shows that you have the ability to reason and make rational judgment.
d. It tells others you are the one that has answers.

C is correct.

People, inmates and officers alike, respond to those that can make rational and reasoned judgments. That is why critical thinking is so important.

What do we call the vocal art of speaking coherently and professional?

a. Resonance
b. Articulation
c. Vociferous
d. Abstract

B is correct.

Articulation is the vocal art of speaking with coherence and professionalism.

Why is patience so important in a prison setting?

a. Have to be patient in all situations with an even measure of skill.
b. It sets the tone that you are in control.
c. It is required that a corrections officer is always patient.
d. It allows for a relaxed environment for everyone.

B is correct.

A patient officer is a controlled officer. A professional officer has to be in control of himself and situations as much as possible.

Why is good health so important?

a. Fitness keeps the mind and body sharp.
b. Fitness allows the officer to respond with readiness.
c. Fitness is important as the job can become physically challenging.
d. All are accurate.

D is correct.

Good health keeps the officer's body and mind sharp, allows him or her to respond with readiness and to aid in physical situations.

Is a sensitive nature important to the job?

a. Yes, as it indicates a willingness to listen.
b. No, because a guard has to be tough at all times.
c. Yes, otherwise you will be the target of future conflict.
d. No, otherwise you become a subject of ridicule.

A is correct.

An officer that has sensitivity is more apt to listen to inmate concerns and questions.

Why is mental stability so important to the position?

a. It defines the officer as a professional.
b. It shows the inmates that you are not prone to mental anguish.
c. Because of the environment, it becomes easy to lose concept of reality.
d. It keeps you from reacting in a vicious or erratic manner when situations arise.

D is correct.

A mentally stable officer will handle situations more controlled and not prone to erratic or vicious behavior.

Criminal law and the Constitution as it Pertains to Correction Officers.

This section will be general questions dealing with criminal law and definitions.

What is a repeat offender?

a. Someone that does the same crime repeatedly.
b. Someone that tries to simulate a crime that someone else commits.
c. Someone that repeatedly commits a crime and is tried and found guilty and incarcerated.
d. There is no such term.

C is correct.

A repeat offender is someone that has been through the criminal justice system a couple of times at least. They consistently do crimes and get incarcerated.

What is meant by concurrent serving of sentences?

a. A sentence that is a first time occurrence.
b. Two sentences requiring back to back incarcerations.
c. Two sentences running at the same time.
d. Two sentences that overlap at some juncture.

C is correct.

Concurrent sentences mean that they are serving two sentences at the same time of their incarceration.

Which of these is not true about a three-strike sentencing?

a. A second strike means sentencing is the same length of time as the first.
b. A third strike is where two prior crimes of serious or violent felonies result in a minimum of life imprisonment, with a 25 year minimum served.
c. A second strike requires twice the sentencing length of the first sentence.
d. A third strike must be of a new violent crime.

A is correct.

The second strike of a three strike sentence means that the sentencing is twice the length of the first one and not the same length of time.

In some states courts, the correctional system will conduct a pre-sentence investigation. What is this?

a.   It is an investigation into the last incarceration period of an inmate.
b.   It is an investigation into the past history of criminal activity to affect a new sentencing.
c.   It is an investigation into police conduct of the recent criminal activity.
d.   It is an investigation to determine prior court behavior.

B is correct.

The pre-sentence hearing will investigate prior criminal activity and sentences, and that will be used to help in determining what new sentence will be assigned.

What is probation?

a. That is where the prison authority declares time served and can release the inmate.
b. That is a term referring to logging good behavior in prison.
c. That is where the convening court determines the length of the sentence.
d. That is where the sentencing court can release a prisoner instead of serving prison time.

D is correct.

Probation is where a sentencing court can release a prisoner under a set of requirements without being sentenced to serve time in jail or prison.

What is meant by parole?

a.   Parole is time given for good behavior.
b.   Parole is where an inmate can be released by an adult parole board for time served.
c.   Parole refers to the court recommending release after incarceration.
d.   Parole is the same thing as probation.

B is correct.

Parole is a shortened sentence approved by a parole board for time served.

In many jurisdictions, what is the minimum sentence for a misdemeanor?

a. Minimum of 18 months.
b. Maximum of 18 months.
c. Minimum of 15 months.
d. Maximum of 15 months.

B is correct.

In many jurisdictions a maximum of 18 months is the sentence for a misdemeanor crime.

What is meant by a felony crime?

a. A crime where the minimum sentence must be more then that of a misdemeanor.
b. A crime where serious bodily harm or death occurred.
c. A crime where theft resulted in an amount higher then an established minimum.
d. All fit the definition of a felony.

D is correct.

Felonies can consist of a sentencing that is longer in duration to that of a misdemeanor. It also can consist of a crime where serious bodily injury or death occurred or a theft of an established minimum dollar amount was committed.

What is the purpose for a correctional facility?

a. It is a place to effect punishment for crimes committed by the inmate.
b. It is a place for an inmate to be prepared for living a law-abiding life after sentence is served.
c. It is solely meant to keep separation of the prisoner from the general public.
d. It is a place for the inmate to consider his actions and accountability.

B is correct.

Correctional facilities main design is for an inmate to hopefully be rehabbed for a life back in society.

Why is a prisoner held in solitary confinement?

a. The inmate crime may be of such nature that their welfare is effected.
b. The inmate is considered to be of a harmful nature to others around him or her.
c. The correctional facility lacks enough space to allow the inmate room elsewhere.
d. Both a and b are correct.

D is correct.

Solitary confinement is a means to protect the inmate being confined due to the nature of his crime and to protect others from being harmed by the inmate.

What is meant by the phrase, "there is honor amongst thieves."?

a. Even criminals have a sense of right and wrong.
b. Certain types of crime are offensive to even inmates.
c. Criminals have no moral conscience.
d. Inmates will not steal from each other.

B is correct.

Honor among thieves means that some crimes are offensive to even the criminal element.

What are Miranda rights?

a. The right to not have to speak unless an attorney is present.
b. The right to speak without an attorney present, whether given notice of Miranda rights or not.
c. The right to refuse not to be spoken to.
d. The right to deny charges being brought forth.

A is correct.

Miranda rights provide for the right to an attorney and to not have to speak without an attorney present. If the person cannot afford an attorney, they will be given one by the courts at no cost.

Do incarcerated prisoners have Miranda rights?

a. No, as they are already incarcerated.
b. Yes, inmates do not have to answer any questions.
c. No, especially if the discussion is about a different crime from the one they were incarcerated for.
d. Yes, they have these rights at all times.

C is correct.

Courts have concluded that since the inmate is already incarcerated, they do not have to be given Miranda rights; especially for a crime that is different from the one that has them incarcerated.

For purposes of Miranda, what two scenarios have to exist to be given Miranda rights?

a. A person has to be in custody and being questioned about the crime in question.
b. A person has to be in custody, but is not being questioned about the crime in question.
c. A person is simply asked to remain, and is being asked about the crime in question.
d. A person is considered under Miranda at all points of a police contact.

A is correct.

Miranda must be given to someone outside of being incarcerated that is in custody and being questioned about the crime being focused upon.

To conduct a cell search of an inmate, do they have any rights?

a.   The inmate has right to an attorney present during a cell search.
b.   The inmate has no expectation of rights.
c.   The inmate must be informed prior to the search that one will occur.
d.   Cells searches cannot be done without a warrant.

B is correct.

Since they are incarcerated, the inmate can have no expectation of rights in regards to their cell being searched.

What is a pat-down search?

a. A quick search for stolen items.
b. A cursory search on a person for any weapons or contraband.
c. A simple search of inmates pockets for weapons or contraband.
d. A search of an inmate's cell.

B is correct.

A pat-down is a simple cursory search of a person from head to toe for any weapons or contraband.

Which Constitutional Amendments guarantee Due process, even for prisoners?

a. The First and Fourteenth
b. The First and Fifth.
c. The Fifth and Fourteenth.
d. The Fifth and Tenth.

C is correct.

The fifth and Fourteenth Amendments refer to due process guarantees, even for prisoners.

How has the First amendment in regards to freedom of speech involved incarcerated inmates?

a. It has no effect on prisoners.
b. It guarantees freedom of speech in mail and conversation, as long as security is not threatened or government processes are not hindered.
c. It guarantees all mail conversation must be left uncensored.
d. It guarantees all forms of conversation have unlimited restraints.

B is correct.

Inmate rights of not having their mail halted or conversation being hindered, as long as security of any form is not threatened or government processes are not hindered, are guaranteed under the First Amendment.

What major right has been extended to prisoners in regards to courts?

a.	The inmate has access to a jailhouse library if one exists.
b.	The inmate must have access to legal counsel at all times.
c.	The inmate may refuse to attend court proceedings.
d.	A and B are correct.

D is correct.

Courts have ruled that inmates have the right to access correctional facility law libraries and must have legal counsel available at all times.

What fundamental right does an inmate have at disciplinary hearings?

a. The right to call witnesses.
b. The right to an attorney present.
c. The right to pick their own jury.
d. The right to excuse plaintiff witnesses.

A is correct.

Inmates have a right to call witnesses at their disciplinary hearings.

Which of these statements is true in regards to the Eighth Amendment?

a. Inmates have the right to be free of attacks from other prisoners.
b. Inmates have a right to equal treatment under medical considerations.
c. Officers may not inflict inappropriate force to resolve a conflict.
d. All are true.

D is correct.

The guarantee of protection to inmates from the 8th Amendment includes the right to be free of attacks from other inmates, right to fair medical treatment and correctional officers may not administer inappropriate force to resolve conflicts.

Answer the next few questions based upon this scenario. They relate to Constitutional rights of a prisoner.

An inmate is caught stealing and has been detained by an officer. The officer begins questioning the inmate without regard to any attorney present. In the course of the verbal interrogation, the inmate exclaims he has a pain and needs to see the prison nurse immediately. The officer denies that request until his interrogation has ended. Meanwhile other officers check the inmate's cell and find other contraband that he has taken and hidden there. One of the punishments put in place is having his mail halted. The inmate is also refused access to any legal advice for the upcoming disciplinary hearing.

What Amendment affects the issue of being detained and questioned?

a. The First amendment for freedom of speech.
b. The Fifth Amendment for right to refuse to cooperate.
c. The Fourteenth for right of due process.
d. No rights have been violated in this matter.

D is correct.

Since the inmate is already incarcerated he has no claim to a right of being free from being detained or interrogated.

What issue has been raised in regards to denied immediate medical attention?

a. No right has been violated in this manner.
b. Eighth in regards to cruel and unusual punishment.
c. Fourteenth for due process.
d. First for freedom of expression.

B is correct.

Denied immediate medical attention when requested falls under the protection of the 8th Amendment in regards to "cruel and unusual" punishment.

What issue is raised in regards to search of his cell?

a. No right has been violated.
b. Fourth for unreasonable search.
c. Fourteenth for due process.
d. Eighth for cruel and unusual punishment.

A is correct.

The inmate has no expectation of any rights with regard to his cell being searched as he is already incarcerated.

What issue is raised in regards to mail being halted?

a. No right has been violated.
b. First for freedom of speech.
c. Fourth for unreasonable search and seizure.
d. Fourteenth for due process.

B is correct.

The inmate cannot have his mail halted as a punishment as it would violate his 1st Amendment rights.

What issue is raised in regards to not being allowed access to legal counsel?

a. No right has been violated.
b. First for freedom of speech.
c. Fourteenth for due process.
d. No Amendments pertain to this issue.

C is correct.

By benefit of the 14th amendment for due process, the inmate must be allowed access to legal counsel.

Can corrections officers conduct pat down searches?

a. Yes, and for any reason.
b. Yes, for contraband and for weapons.
c. No, for any reason.
d. No, unless for purposes of officer safety only.

B is correct.

Correctional officers have the right to conduct pat-down searches for contraband and weapons.

Are correctional facilities exempt from litigation in reference to sexual harassment?

a. No, facilities must do all they can to discipline inmates that provide an atmosphere of sexual harassment towards female officers.
b. Yes, as an inmate cannot be controlled to not act inappropriately.
c. No, as inmates must be prohibited from contacting female officers.
d. Yes, as it is up to the officer to become hardened to such situations.

A is correct.

Courts have ruled that correctional facilities must do what they can to provide an atmosphere free of sexual harassment towards female officers from fellow officers and inmates.

Court Case Turner vs. Safley provided for what in regards to inmates?

a. That the inmate had the right to a hearing with peers present.
b. That the inmate could not be denied Constitutional rights.
c. Inmates must be allowed to a certain amount of phone calls a year.
d. Inmates could not be prevented from seeing an attorney.

B is correct.

Turner v Safley successfully affirmed that an inmate's Constitutional guarantees could not be denied.

Which of these is not an allowable excuse for not providing for inmate rights?

a. Ignorance of existing laws.
b. Inability to properly staff the facility.
c. Lack of funds to provide for basic rights.
d. All of the above.

D is correct.

Courts have ruled that lack of funds, staffing shortage issues or ignorance of the laws would not protect correctional facilities that deny inmates their civil rights.

Sometimes legislative actions occur to loosen the hold of courts upon Prison operations. What is a more notable act that was created?

a. The Prison Liability Act
b. The Penal system Reform act
c. The Prison Litigation Reform Act
d. The Act to Refuse Court Interference.

C is correct.

The Prison Litigation Reform Act loosened what inmates could try to sue for. This was to provide a means of protection for the correctional facilities from useless lawsuits.

From the question above, what did the act in question have the most impact on?

a.   It impacted how inmates can be allowed to have access to legal resources.
b.   It impacted the lowering of civil lawsuits from inmates.
c.   It caused a decrease in the conflicts officers were being involved in.
d.   It caused inmates to begin organized legal meetings.

B is correct.

As explained the Act impacted the lowering the volume of civil lawsuits from inmates.

Does the Americans with Disabilities Act affect prisons?

a. Yes, it requires prisons to provide proper medical access.
b. No
c. Yes, it requires prisoners to have proper wheelchair access to all portions of a facility.
d. A and c are correct.

D is correct.

The ADA requires prisons to provide for proper medical access and for wheelchair access to all relevant portions of a correctional facility.

What is meant by phrase, "under the color of the state law"?

a. Prisons must adopt state funds for running their facilities.
b. Only state run facilities must follow state regulations.
c. Private and state run prisons must follow state regulations.
d. There is no such term.

C is correct.

"Under the color of state law" means that privately and governmentally run state correctional facilities must follow state regulations.

Specifically, in regards to prisons, what does the eighth Amendment oversee?

a. Due process.
b. Search and seizure.
c. Cruel and Unusual Punishment.
d. Right to not incriminate oneself.

C is correct.

The 8th Amendment oversees the issue of "cruel and unusual" punishment in regards to correctional facilities.

What does the Fourteenth Amendment protect in regards to Correctional facilities?

a. Freedom of speech.
b. Due process procedure.
c. Search and Seizure.
d. Right to not incriminate oneself.

The 14th Amendment provides for "due process" in regards to correctional facilities.

Fourth Amendment pertains to what in regards to prisons?

a. Unreasonable search and seizure.
b. Due process procedure.
c. Freedom of Speech.
d. Cruel and unusual punishment.

A is correct.

The 4th Amendment pertains to "Unreasonable search and seizure" issues in regards to correctional facilities.

First Amendment has what protections for inmates?

a. The protection of personal property.
b. The protection of free speech.
c. The protection of not having to incriminate oneself.
d. The protection of personal space.

B is correct.

The First Amendment protects issues of free speech in regards to inmates.

Intake and Screening.

Which of these is true in regards to a prisoner during in-take process?

a.   No special considerations need to be involved for men and women prisoners.
b.   Women must be kept separate from men during the intake process.
c.   Juveniles and adults may be in taken together.
d.   Prior criminal history is never involved during the process of in-take.

B is correct.

Courts have ruled that men and women must be kept separate during the in-take process into correctional facilities.

Why is medical history so important during the in-take process?

a. It is not important.
b. Medical history helps in classifying each inmate in regards to race and age.
c. Medical history has bearing on where an inmate will initially be assigned to.
d. Medical history is simply a means for census purposes.

C is correct.

Medical history will impact where an inmate will be assigned to in the in-take process.

What does a classification system establish?

a.   It establishes where an inmate will end up being housed within the facility.
b.   It establishes proper protocol for handling specific cases.
c.   It enforces the rules of court procedure in establishing levels of punishment.
d.   There is no such thing.

A is correct.

A classification system during in-take will establish where the inmate will be housed within the correctional facility.

What other protocols are met during the classification process?

a. Establishing cell mate selections.
b. Helping to assess security risks.
c. Aiding in the health needs of each inmate.
d. All of the above.

D is correct.

Other protocols to be met during the classification process include cellmate selections, assessing the inmate's security risk and assisting the health needs of each inmate.

Inmate Respect and Dignity.

Courts have established that inmates have a certain level of respect and dignity that needs to be observed by correctional staff. The next few questions will address this issue.

How should inmates be treated by correctional officers?

a. Be respectful at all times.
b. Be respectful unless the inmate has disregarded a lawful order.
c. Respect has to be earned to be observed.
d. Officers are to monitor and control, not respect.

A is correct.

Correctional officers should treat inmates with respect at all times.

How does an officer verbally engage an inmate?

a. Be commanding at all times.
b. Show sensitivity to engender respect.
c. Treat the inmate with dignity when addressing them.
d. Remember that a correctional officer is to be mindful that respect is an inmate by inmate rational.

C is correct.

An officer must verbally engage the inmate with dignity when addressing them.

Which of these is the best way to handle a situation where the inmate is being verbally abusive?

a. Be in control, yet let the inmate see you have a soft side.
b. Respect is all in the voice.
c. To show dignity you speak with authority and fairness.
d. Constantly remind the inmate to just shut-up.

C is correct.

When an inmate is being verbally abusive to an officer, the officer needs to show dignity with authority and fairness.

Which of these is true in regards to officer stress and respect to the inmate?

a. There is no correlation.
b. Officer stress can result in treating inmates cruelly and abusive.
c. Officer stress always remains high so as to be alert.
d. An officer under stress will still need to remain respectful.

B is correct.

An officer under a stressful time may be prone to treat an inmate abusively and cruelly. This is the time an officer needs to show respect towards the inmate.

Court Testimony

Why is it important for an officer to dress professionally in court?

a. The way one dresses has no bearing on how one is judged.
b. An officer dresses professionally to give an air of truth to his testimony.
c. Professional dress coincides with professional conduct in a courtroom.
d. Dressing professional will show the judge your credibility.

C is correct.

Professional dress and professional conduct are both a necessity for a corrections officer involved in a courtroom.

What is the best decorum to handle while in a witness box?

a. Be as relaxed and focused as possible.
b. Remain alert to any illegal activities that may occur in the courtroom.
c. Act as if you are going to answer before the question is asked to demonstrate your efficiency.
d. Be composed and witty to alleviate the tension in the courtroom.

A is correct.

Since a witness box can be an unnerving situation, the officer must be focused and relaxed. This will aid in his demeanor while under examination by attorneys and the judge.

What is the best way to answer the questions presented to an officer on the witness stand?

a. Respond quickly and without hesitation, otherwise they doubt your honesty.
b. Respond with deliberateness and straightforwardness.
c. Respond with a painted picture of the scene or situation, to keep it from being dry.
d. Respond as if your life depended upon your responses.

B is correct.

The best way to respond to questions while on the witness stand is for the officer to answer with deliberateness and be straight forward with answers.

When in the courtroom, who are you actually offering testimony to?

a. To the lawyer asking the question.
b. To the lawyers on both sides of the argument.
c. To the judge, or finder of facts.
d. To the courtroom audience.

C is correct.

An officer in a witness stand is actually offering testimony to the finder of facts, i.e. the judge.

What is meant by leading a witness in questioning from the attorney?

a.   The question is establishing your credibility to answer.
b.   The question is seeking to take you to a pre-designed destination of your answer.
c.   The question is asked to see if you are alert to the question.
d.   The question is totally unbiased.

B is correct.

To lead a witness means the attorney is trying to get you to a pre-designed "place" in regards to your testimony.

When responding to a question, what should your demeanor be?

a. One of aloofness
b. One of focus.
c. One of incredulous
d. One of distain.

B is correct.

Demeanor on the witness stand should be focused at all times. This way the attorney will have a harder time of trying to trap you in your answers to questions.

What does it mean to consider your answer?

a.	It means to give slow and animated responses.
b.	It means to consider if you will tell some of the story or all of it.
c.	It means to consider what is asked and what your response should be.
d.	It means nothing as you would respond quickly.

C is correct.

To consider the answer is to consider what the response to particular questions should be. It means to thoughtfully think through your answer.

Why do you only answer the question and nothing more?

a. Your answer is simply to supply your opinion of what you saw or know.
b. Your response is to give clarity and truth to what is asked.
c. Because some people only answer what they want to answer.
d. There is no such way of thinking in how to answer a question.

B is correct.

Answering only the question is to provide clarity and truth to the question. Some people try to offer more information than what is asked of them.

How should you present yourself when in the witness stand?

a. Present yourself as if you were in control of the courtroom.
b. Present yourself as relaxed as possible and sit slightly slouched in the chair.
c. It doesn't matter what others think of you, you are simply there to answer questions.
d. Present yourself with professional decorum and sit up straight in the chair.

D is correct.

The officer should be sitting straight up and presenting a professional presence.

When asked a question, how do you respond in voice tone?

a. Answer in a yell so those in the back can hear you.
b. Answer softly so as to appear humble.
c. Answer with an audible tone and clarity.
d. Answer with slow and deliberate enunciation of each syllable of each word.

C is correct.

The officer should answer with clarity and an audible tone.

What does it mean by the term "baiting" the witness?

a. Means trying to lead you in the direction of an answer.
b. Means to confuse your answers.
c. Means to try to get the witness upset in their answers.
d. There is no such term with courtroom testimony.

C is correct.

To bait the witness is to try to get the witness upset in their answers. The officer should combat this by remaining calm at all times of questioning.

Why do you avoid looking at your attorney or anyone other then the judge or lawyer asking the questions?

a.   It may appear you are being coached in your answers.
b.   Some may think you are looking for a way out.
c.   It may appear you are bored and refuse to look elsewhere.
d.   It may seem that you feel you are being harassed by the cross-examination.

A is correct.

To look at anyone but the judge when answering questions may give the impression that you are being coached by the person you keep looking at.

What is meant by discovery in a courtroom situation?

a. It means that new evidence has been unearthed.
b. It means that one side's evidence must be made discoverable to the other side.
c. It means that a new witness has been discovered for the trial.
d. It means that a witness's testimony has been discovered to be false.

B is correct.

Discovery means that all sides of the court case have the right of access to all evidence being presented. This should be provided before the court case begins.

What is meant by habeas corpus?

a. The body or the person.
b. The procedure of courtroom behavior.
c. The adjudication of a crime.
d. The selection of a jury.

A is correct.

Habeas Corpus means the body, or person, to be presented at court time.

Memory and Observations.

Listed is a series of actions occurring. Select the answer that best describes the activity.

1. All dirty linen was handed out to the receiving officer.
2. Final head count was taken after the linen activity.
3. Each inmate was directed to leave the area and head to their cell.
4. All doors were locked behind the inmate as they proceeded into their housing cell.
5. The prisoners lined for roll-call.
6. All inmates received linen for making up their beds.

a. 1,4,6,3,5,2
b. 5,6,3,4,1,2
c. 4,2,1,5,3,6
d. 2,4,6,5,3,1

B is correct.

5,6,3,4,1,2 best describes the order of actions that was listed.

Their dirty linen was handed off to whom?

a. linen officer
b. duty officer
c. orderly
d. kitchen officer

A is correct.

The dirty linen was handed off to the linen officer.

Read the following scenario and answer the questions with the appropriate answer.

Inmate M was ordered to go to the cafeteria and relieve Inmate O from dishwashing duties. As he approached the kitchen, Inmate M noticed a piece of metal on the floor and retrieved it. He hid it in his shoe and headed towards the kitchen. Correctional officer A noticed the metal piece extended out of the inmates shoe and ordered him to hand it over. At this time Inmate O used the officer's distracted attention to slip out of a side door. Placing Inmate M in custody of Officer C, Officer A went after and apprehended Inmate O trying to escape out of the unit.

In the whole scenario presented what major mistake was present, or not present?

a. Incomplete number of officers to be present.
b. No officer escorting Inmate M to the kitchen.
c. Inmate O being allowed to exit the kitchen without prior approval.
d. Inmate M finding the piece of metal.

B is correct.

There was no officer escorting Inmate M to the kitchen. That was the major mistake.

What person depicted was working in the kitchen originally?

a. Inmate M
b. Officer C
c. Inmate O
d. Officer A

C is correct.

Inmate O was originally working in the kitchen according to the narrative.

Note: because visual recognition and memory is so important for a corrections officer, the following 3 pictures are to help with practicing these areas. The time spent looking at each picture will increase incrementally based on the volume of pictural content.

What can a good report do for a court case?

Look at the attached picture and answer the following questions after 15 seconds of examination.

The lady standing in the foreground is wearing what over her blouse.

a. A college letter sweater.
b. A plain jacket.
c. A light-colored sweater.
d. Simply her blouse.

A is correct.

The lady standing is wearing a college letter sweater.

The car is best described by which response in the picture?

a. The car is facing left.
b. The car driver side door is open.
c. The car is facing right.
d. The car is a wagon.

C is correct.

According to the picture, the car is facing right.

How many people are in the picture?

a. There are 2 people.
b. There are 2 people standing and one in the car.
c. There are 2 women and one male, which are in the car.
d. There are 2 men standing and one woman in the car.

B is most correct.

According to the picture there are 2 people standing and one in the car.

Who is wearing the hat?

a. The woman in the car.
b. The man outside of the car.
c. The woman outside of the car.
d. No one is wearing a hat.

B is correct.

According to the picture the man outside of the car is wearing the hat.

Look at the picture below for 20 seconds then answer the following questions? Try not to re-look.

In the picture, what is laying on the ground?

a. A ladder on its side.
b. A tree branch.
c. A black hose.
d. A section of fence.

A is correct.

According to the picture a ladder is laying on the ground.

In the back, what is behind the bushes?

a. A dark colored car with brake lights on.
b. A light colored car with no brake lights on.
c. A dark colored car with no brake lights on.
d. A light colored car with brake lights on.

D is correct.

According to the picture, a light colored car with its brake light on is behind the bushes.

There are how many lengths of hose on the ground?

a. There is one length of hose.
b. There are two lengths of hose, same color.
c. There are two lengths of hose, differing colors.
d. There are 3 separate lengths of hose.

C is correct.

According to the picture there are two lengths of hose of differing colors on the ground.

What type of fence is in the background?

a. It is a rod-iron fence.
b. It is a picket fence.
c. It is a wooden split rail fence.
d. There is no fence.

C is correct.

According to the picture the type of fence is a split-rail fence.

Look at the picture below for 25 seconds, and then answer the following questions without referring back to the picture.

In the back ground is something blue. What is it?

a. Part of a map.
b. Part of a display.
c. It is a ribbon.
d. There is no blue.

B is correct.

According to the picture, the blue is part of a display.

How many dinosaur skeletons are in the clearly visible in the picture?

a. 2
b. 3
c. 4
d. 5

A is correct.

According to the picture there are two dinosaur skeletons clearly visible.

How many complete framed pictures are visible in the left hand side of the picture background?

a. 4
b. 5
c. 6
d. 7

C is correct.

According to the picture there are 6 framed pictures visible in the left hand side of the picture.

The list below will list people and their addresses. Answer the next set of questions in relation to this list without trying to look back at the list.

John Smith 8585 Asbury Lane
John A Smith 9765 Elm St
Jane Smith 6767 Walnut Lane
Jane Q Smith 4986 Cherry park Way

Who lives at the non-tree named address?

a. Jane Q Smith
b. Jane Smith
c. John A Smith
d. John Smith

D is correct.

John Smith lives on the non-tree named street.

Who lives at the address that ends in an even number?

a. Jane Q Smith
b. Jane Smith
c. John A Smith
d. John Smith

A is correct.

Jane Q Smith lives at the address that ends in an even number.

John A Smith lives at ___ Elm Street

a. 6767
b. 9765
c. 4986
d. 8585

B is correct.

John A Smith lives at 9765 Elm Street.

What is the street that coordinates to house number 8585?

a. Asbury Lane
b. Elm Street
c. Walnut Lane
d. Cherry Park Way

A is correct.

Asbury Lane is the street that coordinates with house number 8585.

Situational Reasoning

Many times corrections officers are placed in position of having to make determinations over what he or she observes. The decisions you make in regards to the situation will become important to how the inmate is handled or situation is resolved.

Answer the next few questions based upon the narrative.

An inmate constantly gets into trouble. If he is not getting into altercations, he is ignoring directives from other officers. The inmate finally showcases a period of good behavior over a two week period. Believing that he is showing a good faith effort to improve his reputation he asks the officer for a favor. He asks the officer if the officer would take a note to the warden asking for some form of gratuity for his improved behavior.

What is the best response to this situation?

a. To totally ignore the request.
b. Take the note with the promise of getting it to the warden, but simply give it to the duty officer.
c. To spend 10 minutes berating the inmate over the ethics of asking the officer to do that request.
d. To leave his assigned position and get the note to the warden.

A is correct.

The best response is for the officer to totally ignore the request as it violates regulations.

Based on the above scenario, which is the worst response?

D is correct.

The worst response would be for the officer to leave his post just to deliver the note. Until relieved by another officer, the officer may not leave his assigned post.

An inmate has been given direction to leave his cell, so a search can be made for contraband. After the search is conducted, food is discovered that could only have been found in the kitchen, as the inmate works there. The officer interrogates the inmates and finds that the inmate did steal the food, but related he did it simply because he hated to see waste.

a.   Tell the inmate the regulation related to the offense and warn him not to do it again.
b.   Report the incident to the immediate supervisor and have them determine punishment.
c.   Ignore the incident as inmates do it all the time.
d.   Reprimand the inmate for the offense and assign proper punishment.

What is the best response to this situation?

B is correct.

To report the incident to an immediate supervisor is the best response as they are better equipped to handle the discipline.

What is the worst response to this incident?

C is correct.

The worst response is to ignore the incident as other inmates feel the inmate has a special relationship with the officer and it violates regulations that require all incidents be reported.

Diffusion of Hostility

What is the extreme basis for the hostility in a prison environment?

a. Personalities not blending well together.
b. Inmates seeking to find their place in the prison environment.
c. Close quarters for some inmates result in disagreements.
d. Inmates trying to bait the officers into a hostile environment.

C is correct.

The close quarters of inmates causes tension to rise and increases the likelihood of disagreements within the environment.

Which of these is an important factor for a correctional officer in preventing hostile situations?

a. Maintaining an environment where the inmates feel intimidated.
b. Be willing to compromise your position when it is necessary.
c. Establish the rules and determine the inmates will adhere to them.
d. Position yourself with control and a strengthened leadership structure.

D is correct.

To prevent hostile situations, officers need to have the control of the environment and a strong leadership structure in place behind them.

What constitutes a strengthened leadership within the system?

a. Proper training for all involved.
b. Perception of knowing who is in control.
c. Each facility has its own declared structure in place.
d. Knowing the established rules and abiding by them.

A is correct.

Proper training of everyone on staff will develop a strong leadership structure as everyone will know their duties and responsibilities.

Why is it important for the correctional officer to be able to multi-task?

a. The officer has to handle many situations and watch the other inmates.
b. The officer must know how to write a report while watching inmates.
c. The officer has to be able to watch a number of inmates simultaneously.
d. It isn't that important.

A is correct.

Multi-tasking is imperative considering the officer must know what is happening within his cell post and to be able to handle the various situations that will arise.

An officer has to have a certain frame of mentality to prevent hostile situations. What is this mentality?

a. Has to be determined to do what it takes to control the inmates.
b. Must realize he or she is the first respondent and must be ready to act and react.
c. Must be motivated to be focused and watch for signs of unrest.
d. Must know who to contact for assistance when signs of unrest appear.

C is correct.

The officer that stays focused to the environment and watch for red flags of unrest will have a better position to respond to hostile situations. This is the strongest mentality.

Sometimes establishing an intimidating show of force is what is needed. How effective is this?

a. Very effective as it establishes the rule of power from the outset.
b. Somewhat effective in that it maintains a level of authority on the part of the officer.
c. Effective only to the point where other means have not been as effective.
d. Not effective at all.

B is correct.

A show of force on the part of officers will be somewhat effective as it establishes a certain level of authority. It is not the most effective means.

What is one of the problems with a coercive approach towards handling inmates?

a. It makes the officer no better then the inmate.
b. It establishes a lack of respect for the authority in place.
c. It shows a weakness on the part of the officer.
d. It makes the officer look inefficient in his role.

B is correct.

If an officer is prone to being coercive then the respect level for authority begins to weaken. Respect is one of the best tools an officer has on his side.

What is one way correctional facilities try to prevent open hostility in the inmate culture?

a. Rewarding those that obey the rules in front of others.
b. Establishing the fact the officer is in charge and will be obeyed.
c. Practicing acknowledging those that have an assumed mantle of authority over other inmates.
d. Telling the inmates simply to do what they are instructed.

C is correct.

The officer that acknowledges the inmates that have an assumed mantle of authority over other inmates helps to establish a preventative approach to hostile situations from happening.

Many times inmates will respond better to an officer that seems confident in his demeanor and duties. Why?

a. The officer represents the prison and assumes a mantle of authority.
b. Inmates feel this officer will be fair and not abuse his authority.
c. There is no such view in the prison system.
d. The officer shows he or she will not be intimidated.

B is correct.

Inmates find that officers that appear confident are usually fair in how they deal with the inmate population. They are less likely to approach inmates with an abusive posture.

A good officer knows to use confidence and force practically. How is this done?

a. The officer realizes their ability is based upon experience.
b. The two aspects work together because the inmate sees it that way.
c. No officer knows how to balance this skill.
d. This only works when the officer has to use it.

A is correct.

A good officer with experience knows how to present a confident demeanor. They also understand that force has to be used with judgment and control.

Do rewards that an officer can issue work for maintaining order?

a. It works as far as the inmates in authority will allow it.
b. It never works.
c. It works for benefit of those that receive the reward.
d. It works when other inmates feel they may earn the reward as well.

D is correct.

It will only work if inmates feel that they can earn rewards as well. If the officer appears to be partial to certain inmates than they decrease the level of keeping order. Respect is key, as is fairness.

What is wrong with the reward mentality?

a. It gives an appearance of weakness on the part of the officer.
b. It makes the inmates feel that some are treated better than others.
c. No officer can give special favors.
d. Rewards diminish effective authority.

A is correct.

A reward mentality makes an officer seem weak to inmates. The inmates feel that officer does not have confidence in his own abilities and traits.

What is a hostile environment?

a. An environment where officers feel that their safety is in danger.
b. An environment where tensions rise within the inmate population.
c. An environment that cultivates anger and distrust.
d. An environment that causes others to force the hand of authority.

C is correct.

A hostile environment is one that fosters anger and distrust among inmates.

The strongest item an officer has to maintain order is what?

a. The fear inmates have of the officer.
b. The admiration that inmates have of the officer.
c. The concern the inmates have for the officer's well-being.
d. The respect the inmates have for the officer.

D is correct.

The strongest tool an officer has on his side to deal with inmates and to maintain order is the respect they have for him or her.

What is meant by "fear" on the part of an inmate when dealing with hostility?

a. The inmate is afraid of everyone.
b. The inmate has fear of being hurt in any way.
c. The inmate fears the officers and what they represent.
d. The inmate knows no fear and that is why they are acting this way.

B is correct.

"Fear" among inmates in hostile situations is the fear of being hurt or killed.

How does an officer handle this fear the inmate is experiencing to dissolve a potential issue?

a. By talking softly and slowly approaching them.
b. By being as animated as the inmate, but projecting a confidence.
c. By rushing straight on into the situation to diffuse it.
d. By ignoring them and tell them to simply settle down.

B is correct.

The officer must be as animated as the hostile inmate, matching his motions, but maintaining confidence at the same time. A silent approach will not work.

Some inmates create situations when they feel their boundaries are being destroyed. What is meant by boundaries?

a. The four walls of their cell.
b. The boundaries of their everyday life in the facility.
c. The boundaries of their mind.
d. The boundaries that officers project upon the inmate.

B is correct.

Boundaries to an inmate mean the boundaries or walls of their everyday existence in incarceration. These boundaries are very real to them as it is a constant with them.

Sometimes the best way to handle a potential crisis is to ignore it. This means what?

a.   Simply to tell the inmate when they calm down you will start to listen to them.
b.   Means to literally ignore them.
c.   Means to wait and watch.
d.   Means you will get some help and during this time the inmate is ignored.

A is correct.

To ignore potential crisis means to let the inmate in question know you will listen when they calm down, otherwise you will "ignore" their remarks.

When should the officer become physically involved?

a. When the inmate begins to get verbally out of control.
b. When the inmate becomes intimidating.
c. When there is an actual attempt by the inmate to make a physical threat.
d. When the inmate starts calling for assistance from other inmates.

C is correct.

An officer becomes physically involved when the inmate commences an actual physical threat.

Some inmates seem to be habitually angry. How are they handled?

a. They should be separated from other inmates so as not to create bad situations.
b. They should be watched with a careful eye.
c. They need to be punished consistently for this behavior.
d. There is no such inmate.

A is correct.

Habitually angry inmates should be separated from other inmates to keep them from becoming hostile situations.

Sometimes inmates will try to intimidate the officer with threats. What is the best response?

a. Counter with a statement that implies the inmate may not like the response.
b. Tell the inmate they are making a fool of themselves in front of everyone.
c. Immediately respond with incarcerating the inmate in a holding cell.
d. Approach them to make them back off.

A is correct.

Sometimes the best way to respond to an inmate that threatens the officer is by telling the inmate they might not like the response. This does not give a specific recourse but puts a question into the inmate's mind.

How often do inmates back-up a threat?

a. Not very often.
b. Sometimes to see what the response will be.
c. Usually consistent so as not to lose respect of their peers.
d. Constantly as it is in their nature.

A is correct.

Most inmates talk more than they follow through with threats.

What is a primary reason for having added assistance in dealing with inmates?

a. The fact that inmates respond to numbers without getting into altercations.
b. So that at the end of the day, the officer can go home.
c. To prove that might makes right.
d. To keep this from happening again.

B is correct.

The primary concern with all correctional facilities is officer safety. By providing added assistance, the officers stand a better chance of not being injured or killed.

When an inmate makes legitimate threat of violence, what should your first response be?

a. Get additional aid.
b. Throw yourself at the inmate.
c. Tell the inmate to go pound sand.
d. Pull out your baton and take a stance.

A is correct.

When an inmate makes a legitimate threat, call for back-up. Officer safety is key, as is protecting other inmates.

Criminal Activity and Case Work within Prisons

Although incarcerated, inmates still live within a world of criminal activity. The corrections officer is the law enforcement individual within the correctional facility and as such has to know how to handle investigations and follow-up procedure.

What forms of crime can exist within the confines of a prison?

a. Drug trafficking.
b. Murder for hire.
c. Theft and robbery.
d. All of the above.

D is correct.

Drugs, murder and theft/robbery can exist within the inmate culture as crimes.

What happens if a crime is committed by an inmate while incarcerated?

a. Time served is automatically taken into account.
b. It becomes a new crime and open to investigation, trial and new sentencing.
c. Nothing as the inmate is already incarcerated.
d. It depends upon the prison authority.

B is correct.

A crime committed by an inmate is treated as a new crime and is open to investigation, trial and new sentencing.

What is meant by investigations of criminal activity within the penal system?

a. Same as in standard police investigations.
b. To find the perpetrator, the evidence and the witness statements.
c. To provide enough information and evidence to bring it to the district attorney.
d. All of the above.

D is correct.

Investigations in prisons are treated just like standard police investigations. Evidence is collected, witness statements are gathered, a perpetrator is sought after and all is presented to the district attorney who will decide on the next move.

Can a correctional officer make an arrest in the prison?

a. Yes in all situations.
b. Yes as they are sworn peace officers.
c. Only with states and jurisdictions that give that parameter.
d. No.

C is correct.

Only states and jurisdictions that give correctional officers arrest powers can make an actual arrest in correctional facilities.

What does it mean to contaminate a crime scene?

a. To leave your own fingerprints on evidence.
b. To leave anything or move anything from the original position of the crime scene.
c. To bring in anything that is not part of the original crime scene.
d. To disturb anything that relates to the crime.

B is correct.

To contaminate a crime scene is to disturb any kind of potential evidence or to leave anything that was not part of the original crime scene.

Why should the fewest of hands handle anything considered evidence?

a. Fewer the hands, least likely to drop and break.
b. Fewer the hands, less likely to contaminate the integrity of the evidence.
c. Fewer the hands, better the likelihood of conviction.
d. Does not matter how many hands handle evidence.

B is correct.

The fewer hands that handle evidence the less likely the integrity of the evidence will be contaminated.

Why does a correctional officer have a better chance of getting results in criminal investigations within prisons?

a. Does not matter.
b. The correctional officer that conducts an investigation has access to inmates to ask questions.
c. The correctional officer understands how to handle the inmates being investigated.
d. The correctional officer can provide favors for inmates willing to cooperate.

C is correct.

A correctional officer may make the best investigator for a crime within the facility as they have access to the inmates on a daily basis and know them better than others would.

Can evidence gathered from the search of an inmate's cell be used in a criminal investigation?

a. Yes
b. No
c. Only if it proves to be part of the crime in question.
d. Only if found with a search warrant.

C is correct.

The potential evidence from an inmate's cell can be part of criminal investigation if it proves to be part of the crime.

What is meant by case management?

a.	Each case of an incident occurring that provides statistics and facts.
b.	Each inmate's records are reviewed and analyzed in aiding their rehabilitation in prison.
c.	Each inmate is considered a case study.
d.	There is no such activity in the penal system.

B is correct.

Case management means to review and analyze inmate's records to aid in their rehabilitation from prison.

Studies show that many inmates fall into recidivism, or return to prison, once released. Why?

a. The original period of incarceration and rehabilitation did not work.
b. The nature of people is to repeat what they commit.
c. No one offered the person adequate attention while incarcerated.
d. Accountability through probation is weak.

A is correct.

Inmates tend to come back to prison because their original time incarcerated was not successful in rehabilitating the inmate.

What is the most used form of case management technique to aid in inmates becoming less likely to return?

a. Looking at the inmate as a person and treating them as such.
b. Establishing a look at the environment the person comes from and aids them in altering that environment.
c. It is up to the inmate to a productive member of society.
d. A reward system for each time the person makes progress.

B is correct.

The most used form of case management is to look at an inmate's environment of where they came from and try to change that environment. This may be done by not going back to where they came from.

How does the correctional officer fit into the case management aspect?

a. The officer has direct contact with the inmate and can have a positive influence.
b. The officer is merely there to make sure the inmate is safe and being watched.
c. The officer maintains daily notes and provides case workers with that information.
d. The case officer is not a part of this program.

A is correct.

The officer has direct contact with the inmate and can be a positive influence.

What are community corrections?

a. It is a system for inmates to become a labor force in the community.
b. Usually based with those on parole to help them integrate into society in a supervised fashion.
c. A system where members of the community come into the correctional facility and observe inmate activity.
d. A means for inmates to participate in community affairs.

B is correct.

Community corrections are where inmates on parole are monitored to help them integrate back into society.

Why is case work management even a necessity in penal systems?

a. Inmates have treated each other so violently that a change was needed.
b. Inmates have felt mistreated and the situation required it.
c. There is no need for it.
d. Inmates have proven time and time again that they will fight the system.

B is correct.

Case work management is a necessity for penal systems to aid those inmates that feel mistreated.

What is the intended purpose of community corrections?

a. Opportunity for inmates to prepare and not return to prison.
b. To create more job opportunities for inmates.
c. To aid facilities in lowering their inmate numbers.
d. To provide a safe atmosphere for the correctional officer.

A is correct.

Community corrections are used to help inmates prepare for life on the outside and not return to prison.

What is one benefit that has come from the formation of case management?

a. Inmates receive better medical attention.
b. Inmates have better food.
c. Inmates have access to educational services.
d. There has been no benefit.

C is correct.

One major benefit for the formation of case management is the access inmates have to educational opportunities.

Critical Incident Stress Management (CISM)

This is an issue that has become pertinent to correctional officers only recently. Jurisdictions may require officers to come with this in relation to their work and how to handle it.

In layman's terms what is Critical Incident Stress Management?

a.	It is the handling of stress brought on by inmate hostility.
b.	It is the working with government agencies and the stress that accompanies it.
c.	It is an aid in helping a person deal with a severe or traumatic incident or situation.
d.	It does not exist.

C is correct.

CISM is an aid to help officers deal with traumatic situations they have encountered and how it affects their life. It allows them to respond to the incident in question and get past it.

How does CISM work?

a.   The corrections officer begins to see a psychiatrist.
b.   The inmate journals the incident and continues to write about his or her thoughts.
c.   The officer talks about it with someone, including another officer.
d.   The officer is placed on a regimen of getting back into the work immediately.

C is correct.

CISM provides opportunity for the officer to discuss the situation that occurred with someone, maybe even another officer as they can identify.

What type of situation can cause the trauma?

a. The death of a colleague.
b. The suicide of someone close.
c. Someone receiving extreme bodily injury because of the officer's actions.
d. All of the above can cause this trauma.

D is correct.

Trauma can be caused by someone dying, someone that they know committing suicide, or the officer being the reason someone else received serious bodily injury.

What are considered the two D's of CISM?

a. Defuse and declare.
b. Declare and Debrief.
c. Defuse and Debrief.
d. Defuse and Debate.

C is correct.

The two D's in CISM are defuse and debrief.

Once a person has been initially dealt with after a traumatic event, how long before the debriefing should occur?

a. 24 hours
b. 72 hours
c. 48 hours
d. Almost immediately afterwards.

B is correct.

Studies indicate the debriefing should occur within 72 hours after the traumatic incident occurred.

Why does CISM seem to work better for correctional officers rather than victims?

a. The officer is more of a witness or not always directly affected whereas the victim is.
b. Victims tend to take longer to respond.
c. The officer is trained to handle extreme situations.
d. The victim has monetary motivation.

A is correct.

Correctional officers seem to respond to CISM better because they are a witness to the event and not a direct participant. That minor detachment can offer a better regimen for success.

Hostage Situations

What might spark a hostage situation?

a. Inmates see opportunity to try and gain attention to their situation.
b. Inmates are feeling unduly harassed and use this as a means to outlet their frustration.
c. An officer makes a critical mistake and puts himself in harms way.
d. All are true.

D is correct.

Inmates that see an opportunity for attention feel unduly harassed and may use this as a means to vent frustration, or an officer that makes a critical mistake and comes into a place of being harmed can spark a hostage situation.

How should an officer handle a hostage situation?

a. Threaten the hostage taker with immediate retaliation.
b. Assure the hostage everything will be fine.
c. Tell the hostage taker they should rethink what they are doing.
d. B and C are correct.

D is correct.

The officer needs to provide assurance to the hostage and to remind the hostage taker they need to re-think what they are doing. These are ways for an officer to handle a hostage situation.

In event that an officer is taken hostage, how should they respond first thing?

a. Remain calm and think logically.
b. Tell the hostage taker that they are making a big mistake and that they better let him go.
c. Devise distraction ideas and make a quick break for freedom.
d. Deliberately focus on insulting the intelligence of the hostage taker.

A is correct.

An officer that is taken hostage needs to maintain calmness and to think logically. They may be the only form of sanity or reason present in the situation.

What is another sound practice to observe if taken hostage?

a. Evaluate to see if you can rush the perpetrator.
b. Focus on details and make mental notes.
c. Start yelling for assistance.
d. Remind the hostage taker that you are an authority and need to be treated as such.

B is correct.

Another thing for an officer to do if taken hostage is to focus on the surroundings and details. Mental note taking is important as well.

Occupational Safety and Health

With the rise in interest for safety in the workplace and the litigation growth that has come from it, more correctional facilities are adding this to their training programs.
These questions will focus on aspects of workplace safety and the Occupational Safety and Health Act as it pertains to correctional facilities.

Some of the issues with health and safety in the prisons are blood related. Why?

a. The volume of people in the prisons makes the likelihood of injuries high.
b. The conflicts that occur create a high level of blood cross-contamination if protective gloves are not used by officers.
c. It is as normal as any other institution or company.
d. There is no concern.

B is correct.

If gloves are not used there becomes a high level of being contaminated by someone else's blood. This may arise from the volume of hostile activities that can occur in the facility.

What is a blood-borne pathogen?

a. A disease carried by blood.
b. A disease that starts in the blood.
c. A blood carrying organism.
d. A blood related disorder.

A is correct.

Disease carried by blood is a blood-borne pathogen.

Why does OSHA pertain to correctional facilities?

a. The act refers to all workplaces.
b. Because prisons fall under federal guidelines.
c. Because OSHA covers all private industry and federally run agencies.
d. Because prisons and jails are notoriously dangerous places to work.

C is correct.

Correctional facilities fall under OSHA because OSHA covers all private industry and federally run agencies.

Another area of OSHA concern is workplace violence. Why in correctional facilities?

a. The need to provide for quality onsite medical care in case of injuries.
b. The need for proper training to minimize the level or frequency of injuries that arise from altercations.
c. The accessibility to the creation or theft of makeshift weapons.
d. All of the above.

D is correct.

OSHA covers various aspects of workplace safety. In so doing they are the regulatory agency that promotes the need for proper medical care in environments where violent activities occur. Through proper training to minimize the level or frequency of injuries, OSHA performs another duty.

How important is the issue of sanitation in regards to OSHA and correctional facilities?

a. None at all.
b. Extremely important as the constant movement, personal hygiene and food consumption by large populations effect sanitation.
c. Only to the point of daily hygiene.
d. Only where inmates are concerned.

B is correct.

Correctional facilities are a feeding ground for unsanitary conditions. Through inmate and staff activities, the need for proper hygiene for inmates, and the volume of food consumption that occurs in prisons, OSHA requirements for healthy and sanitary conditions come into play.

How important is OSHA to correctional officers directly?

a. Very important because of the inmate activity and other activities happening in the correctional facility.
b. Not important.
c. Only if a workplace incident directly involves the officer.
d. Only if OSHA sees a problem.

A is correct.

Officer safety becomes a concern for OSHA requirements in relation to the officer's contact with a population that is prone to violence towards those in authority.

Suicide Awareness and Prevention

Due to the stress level facing many corrections officers and dealing with a population that would like to cause physical harm to the officer on a daily basis, the issue of suicide awareness becomes relevant. Many correctional institutions are bringing this issue into play with their training programs. It is also a necessity for officers to have training on focus on the possibility of suicide with inmates as well.

What is a common excuse made in regards to correctional officers and inmate suicide awareness?

a. If someone wants to end their life they will find a way.
b. The officer cannot read everyone's mind.
c. Everything that could be done was done.
d. All of the above.

D is correct.

Various excuses exist in regards to obstacles for officers and inmates in regards to suicide. Someone will find a way that wants to, the officer cannot read minds, everything that could be done was done are all examples of these types of excuses.

What is considered a most effective means of handling the above mentioned excuses in dealing with suicide awareness?

a. Open your eyes to the problem.
b. Attitude in the officers
c. Look for warning signs.
d. None of the above.

B is correct.

The attitude officers possess towards suicide and the signs of suicide among the inmates is considered a most effective tool for correctional officers in how they deal with suicidal awareness.

If awareness is going to improve, what factor about an inmate should be stressed?

a. The history of inmates prone to suicidal tendencies is made known to officers.
b. The look an inmate has in day to day life.
c. The relationship inmates carry on with others.
d. The inmate's personal attitude.

A is correct.

The history of an inmate in regards to suicidal tendencies is a main factor that needs to be stressed in relation towards improving suicide awareness.

Which of these situations is a statistical fact about inmates prone to suicide?

a. They have recent history of open hostility.
b. They prefer to be loners.
c. The suicide occurred while housed alone.
d. The inmate's personal space was being violated.

C is correct.

Inmates that were housed in a cell alone from other inmates were when many suicides occurred. This was based on statistics.

What would be a strong reason suicide among correctional officers is a real concern?

a. The day to day world the correctional officer deals with.
b. The value of life is cheap among the people the officer has to watch over everyday.
c. Problems at home carry over into the workplace.
d. Both B and C are true.

D is correct.

Correctional officers see life being valued as a cheap commodity within the inmate culture they witness on a daily basis. This factor matched with home problems being brought to the workplace added to the suicidal tendencies of these officers.

What is a true factor in regards to suicide awareness and prevention?

a. The solution is dealing with individual situations.
b. The solution is when it is treated as a constant concern.
c. The solution lies on the shoulders of psychologists.
d. The solution happens with more money being spent on the problem.

B is correct.

When suicidal awareness is treated as a constant concern, and not as a once in a while event, then positive solutions have an improved chance of being successful.

In regards to handling inmate suicides, what is a good reference point to begin with?

a. At the point of intake into the facility.
b. At the point the inmate begins to share his or her concerns.
c. At the point the officer witnesses anything out of the ordinary.
d. All of the above.

A is correct.

Knowing that a prisoner has a potential history of suicidal attempts at the point of in-take into the correctional facility is a good starting point in dealing with suicide in relation to that individual.

What becomes a quality help in regards to correctional officer suicide prevention?

a. When peers and colleagues become a support group.
b. When authority realizes that the hours are too long.
c. When the officer feels he or she needs to change their attitude.
d. When the officer quits being negative.

A is correct.

When an officer's peers and fellow officers provide a support system, the officer is provided with a good resource towards help in regards to his or her own suicidal awareness.

Based on the facts and statistics, what is important in dealing with suicide with inmates and fellow officers?

a. Willingness to watch and be aware.
b. Attitude.
c. Stop worrying about everything.
d. A and B are true

D is correct.

The attitude officers possess and the willingness to watch for warning signs all aid in suicidal awareness, with officers and inmates alike.

What program would be a benefit for correctional officers dealing with issues that can lead to suicidal thoughts?

a. A peer group.
b. Critical Stress management
c. Community groups.
d. A and B are valid.

D is correct.

Critical Incident Stress management is a valuable program to aid officers that might be dealing with thoughts of suicide.

Gangs

The awareness that gang activity exists in correctional facilities is an important part of the officer's routine.

Gang activity is very real in correctional facilities. Why is there a concern when using the term gang with certain entities?

a. By changing the name, inmates are not apt to become a part of the group.
b. By changing the name, efforts to halt the activity improve.
c. Changing the name keeps critics of prison systems from gaining an upper hand.
d. It is the preferred way for correctional authorities to designate the problem.

D is correct.

Correctional authorities prefer to not give credence to the term gangs. They prefer to regard these groups as Security Threat groups.

What is the culture of gangs like in correctional facilities?

a. Quite different from the activity of gangs outside of prisons.
b. Quite similar to the activity of gangs outside of prisons.
c. It is a low priority issue.
d. Gangs inside correctional facilities are more like clubs.

B is correct.

Gangs inside and outside of correctional facilities tend to resemble each other in their criminal activities.

Statistics have gang activity having approximately what percentage of crime within correctional facilities?

a. Over 20 percent of all crimes inside of facilities.
b. Over 30 percent.
c. Over 40 percent.
d. None

C is correct.

Based on averages of various states, criminal activity in correctional facilities makes up over 40 percent being done by gangs.

What is one way gangs tend to maintain the "loyalty" of members?

a. The very threat of violence towards family members and gang members
b. Promise to reward the member well for activities performed.
c. Threat of exposing the person to authorities.
d. None of the above.

A is correct.

Gangs tend to establish a form of loyalty by threats of violence towards gang members and their families.

Gangs, or Security Threat groups, are defined as what?

a. Any group of people formed to create an atmosphere of harassment.
b. A group whose main focus is to cause disruptive or threatening behavior.
c. Any group formed to overthrow the convening authority.
d. None of the above.

B is correct.

A group whose focus is to cause disruptive or threatening behavior is the definition of a gang.

What inmate population is conducive to recruitment into gangs?

a. Those that are already gang members on the outside of facilities.
b. New inmates looking for acceptance.
c. Juveniles easily impressed and/or threatened.
d. All of the above.

D is correct.

Gangs find potential members from former gang members, new inmates and juveniles. Obviously the juvenile situations occur in juvenile detention centers.

What other problems do gangs bring to correctional facilities?

a. They create a problem for others that do not want to become part of the gang.
b. They draw so much attention to themselves; other inmates are ignored in regards to criminal activity.
c. They try to incite the riots that occur.
d. They create no other problem.

A is correct.

Another problem gangs bring into correctional facilities is the harassment upon inmates that choose not to become part of the gang culture.

What type of criminal activity do gangs inside of Correctional facilities perform?

a. Drugs
b. Theft
c. Physical violence.
d. All of the above.

D is correct.

Gangs perform the same types of crimes in correctional facilities that gangs outside the system do; drugs, theft/robbery, and violence.

Are correctional facility gangs able to influence crime on the outside?

a. No they do not have that ability.
b. Only to the point of petty crime.
c. Yes, through threat of violence they can perform a major crime.
d. None of the above.

C is correct.

Gangs inside of correctional facilities can operate crime outside by threatening violence upon members families or upon the member that is inside of prison. They do the later to intimidate family members to commit a crime since they are outside of the prison.

A program dealing with gang members, called The Security Threat Group management, exists in some jurisdictions. How effective is it?

a. None whatsoever.
b. It has lowered the level of returning members back to gang cultures.
c. It has worked by threats of constant observation.
d. It works when the funds are available.

B is correct.

The Security Threat Group management program has lowered the recidivism rate of many former gang members as compared to those that do not participate.

Another way of dealing successfully with correctional facility gang issues is what?

a. By changing the housing units of career members thus separating them from others.
b. By a constant surveillance of activities.
c. By threatening the primary members with lengthened lock-ups.
d. By denying mail privileges.

A is correct.

When career gang members are separated from other gang members, by changing their housing cells, their effectiveness to perform gang activity has been affected.

MAR 2014

CLIFTON PARK-HALMOON PUBLIC LIBRARY, NY

0 00 06 04291880

TWO WEEK LOAN

8849898R00360

Made in the USA
San Bernardino, CA
27 February 2014